Other titles by Ian Falloon

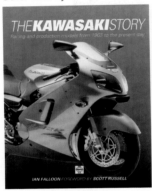

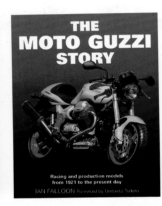

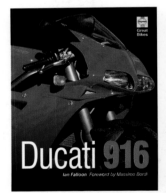

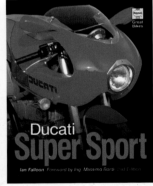

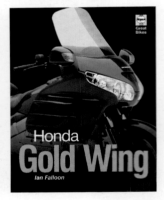

Kawasaki
R A C E R S

ROAD-RACING MOTORCYCLES FROM 1965 TO THE PRESENT DAY **IAN FALLOON** FOREWORD BY **KORK BALLINGTON**

First published in 2002

A catalogue record for this book is available from the British Library

ISBN 1 85960 831 0

Library of Congress catalog card no. 2001099278

Published by Haynes Publishing, Sparkford,
Yeovil, Somerset BA22 7JJ, England

Tel: 01963 442030 Fax: 01963 440001
Int. tel: +44 1963 442030 Fax: +44 1963 440001
E-mail: sales@haynes-manuals.co.uk
Web site: www.haynes.co.uk

Haynes North America, Inc.,
861 Lawrence Drive, Newbury Park,
California 91320, USA

Printed and bound in England by J. H. Haynes & Co. Ltd, Sparkford

CONTENTS

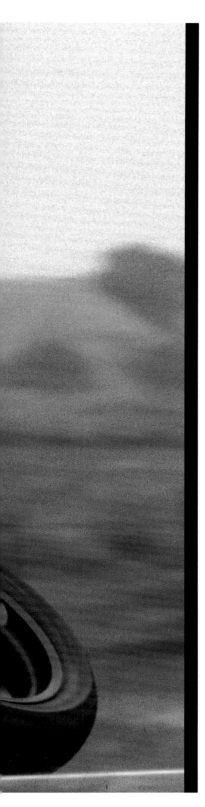

Kork Ballington on his way to seventh place in the 1982 500cc Dutch TT. On this third version of the KR500 Ballington won the British 500cc Championship and very nearly won the British Grand Prix, but for brake problems. *(Mick Woollett)*

FOREWORD BY
KORK BALLINGTON

Whenever I think of Kawasaki's road racing effort I think of the underdog, the smaller of the Japanese giants making headway against the financial might of their opponents. Size relates to budget and since Kawasaki first ventured into road racing in 1965 I believe they have been beset by the constraints of insufficient budget to make the most of their engineers' true genius. There have been a few examples of when they have struck the right chord, and the astounding results were indicative of their capabilities with the basic design on occasion being capable of winning for many years.

My personal experience with the marque started in 1970 on an H1 in production class racing in South Africa. I won the 1972 South African Unlimited Championship aboard an H1-R and in 1973 and 1974 I raced a homebrewed H2 Seeley very successfully in England and Europe. Our decision as a team to use Kawasakis was brought about by the fact that they were affordable and fast! I had a brief flirtation with H2-Rs in the first half of 1975 but by then they were outpaced and I would not get on another lime green bike until 1978 when Kawasaki signed me up to ride the incredible KR250 and KR350 Grand Prix thoroughbreds. The three prototype KR500s that followed in 1980, '81 and '82 were amazing and a tribute to Kawasaki's engineering ability. Despite no pre GP testing these unique and beautifully engineered machines had notable success against better funded and more established teams in the 500cc class.

Ian Falloon's book is an excellent and interesting summary of the highs and lows of Kawasaki's racing efforts since 1965. It is a privilege and honour for me to be mentioned alongside the great riders who are a part of the story and to have been associated with such a great marque.

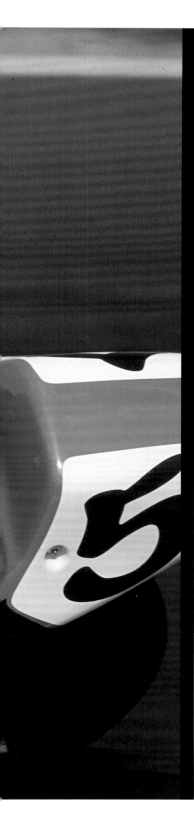

From 1997 until 2001 Akira Yanagawa was Kawasaki's leading rider in the World Superbike Championship.
(Ian Falloon)

INTRODUCTION
AND ACKNOWLEDGEMENTS

As the smallest of the Japanese motorcycle manufacturers, road racing for Kawasaki has never been as important as it has been for Honda, Yamaha, or Suzuki. Given this, and considering the limited emphasis and resources, the results achieved by Kawasaki on the race track since 1969 are totally out of proportion to the level of commitment. Kawasaki has tended to adopt a more European approach to racing development through the constant evolution of a design, and because of this, they have often managed to defeat seemingly more advanced competition. Rather than direct factory involvement Kawasaki has also often left it to enthusiastic and talented individuals to shoulder their racing burden. This is a story of those people as much as it is of the motorcycles.

With so much of this racing history now in the distant past, I couldn't have completed this project without the cooperation of some of the most important Kawasaki riders and tuners. This includes Kawasaki World Champions Kork Ballington, Anton Mang and Scott Russell, and factory riders Barry Ditchburn, Robbie Phillis, Murray Sayle, Paul Smart, Hurley Wilvert and Akira Yanagawa. Bob Hansen recalled the days of Team Hansen in the USA, while Neville Doyle and Peter Doyle provided detailed information on over two decades of preparing Kawasaki racing machinery. With the assistance of Phil Smith and Harald Eckl I was able to obtain details of the current factory World Superbike programme.

Through access to the photographic archives of Mick Woollett, and the magazines of *Cycle World*, *Two Wheels* and *Australian Motorcycle News*, I was fortunate to obtain many previously unpublished photographs. My thanks go to Mick Woollett and the respective magazine editors David Edwards, Jeremy Bowdler and Ken Wootton. Others who have helped were Dave Crussell, Roy Kidney and Darryl Reach, and I would especially like to thank Kork Ballington for agreeing to write the foreword. Of course, none of this would have been possible without the support of my family.

Ian Falloon

1 DAVE SIMMONDS AND KAWASAKI'S FIRST WORLD TITLE

Works rider Toshio Fujii with the 125cc Grand Prix racer at its European debut at the German Grand Prix in May 1966. One month later he died during practice at the Isle of Man. *(Mick Woollett)*

Kawasaki only began building complete motorcycles under their own brand name in 1963, but it wasn't long before they ventured into the world of road racing. Racing was highly regarded as an effective advertising medium, and with Honda and Suzuki dominating the domestic racing scene, Kawasaki built a 125cc liquid-cooled rotary valve two-stroke twin during 1965. This they ambitiously expected to be competitive in the 1965 Japanese Grand Prix, but it was completely out-classed. Undeterred, Kawasaki then decided to develop an air-cooled 125cc disc-valve twin, this initially being offered to British rider Dave Simmonds to race in the Spanish, West German, Isle of Man, and Dutch TTs. However, problems with the air-cooled prototype saw a return to liquid cooling, and Dave Simmonds without a bike for 1966.

Development of the new eight-speed water-cooled twin-cylinder 125cc machine proceeded quickly, and for the second Grand Prix of 1966, at Hockenheim, Kawasaki entered their own rider, Toshio Fujii. Fujii had previously ridden a Suzuki, in Britain as well as Japan, and was considered one of Japan's best riders. It was a very promising debut and although Fujii crashed in practice, he was holding down sixth place in the race before retiring. After returning to Japan, a month later the team travelled to the Isle of Man TT where tragic-ally, Fujii was killed in practice. He fell at Cruickshanks Corner, Ramsey, and suffered internal injuries.

In addition to riding the 125cc Kawasaki, Dave Simmonds was also the mechanic. He is seen here working on the engine at the 1969 Finnish Grand Prix at Imatra. He won the race, which was his sixth in succession. *(Mick Woollett)*

DAVE SIMMONDS

Born on 25 October 1940, Dave Simmonds came from a family with a passion for motorcycles. His father John received a 350cc Douglas from his bride Violet as a wedding present and as soon as the young Dave left school he had his sights set on racing motorcycles. Both Dave and his elder brother Mike were racing ageing 50cc Itoms when a breakthrough came in 1962. John Simmonds, working as an air steward on the BOAC service to Japan found a single-cylinder 50cc Tohatsu Runpet in Tokyo. Both the Simmonds brothers raced this with considerable success, culminating in Tohatsu sending them a pair of new, twin-cylinder 50cc and 125cc two-stroke racers for the 1963 season. These machines

proved sensational, and Dave finished the 1963 season as winner of the 125cc ACU Star.

Pleased with this result, Tohatsu invited Dave to Japan to race in the 1963 Japanese Grand Prix. Here, he finished 13th in the 50cc race but retired in the 125, fully expecting this would lead to a factory ride in Europe during 1964. Unfortunately, Tohatsu went into bankruptcy, leaving Dave to race the 1963 machines, along with a couple of Honda twins he found in Japan. The following year and 1965 were difficult, culminating in a crash at Mallory Park in September 1965, breaking his ankle. Recovering in hospital, he received a call offering him a works 125cc Kawasaki for four selected classic events during 1966.

Simmonds came to Kawasaki's attention through Atsushi Yokohama who had worked at Tohatsu before moving to Kawasaki, but it wasn't until October 1966 that he finally got to ride the Kawasaki. Along with Chris Vincent, Simmonds was invited to race a factory 125cc twin at the Japanese Grand Prix at Fuji. Dave finished an unremarkable eighth but this led to discussion regarding a contract for 1967. The only problem was the factory could only afford to supply a motorcycle and no mechanic. Simmonds then told Kawasaki that he was more than able to prepare the machine himself, and he returned to complete a three-week course in the racing department. Convinced of his competence, Kawasaki agreed to supply Simmonds with a 125 and an A1R.

After clinching the 1969 125 World Championship in Belgium, Dave rushed back to England to marry Julie Boddice. Hailing from another motorcycle racing dynasty, Julie's father Bill was many times British sidecar champion, and her brother Mick later continued the sidecar tradition. Unfortunately, Dave's life met a tragic end in 1972. On 23 October, at a one-off meeting held in Rungis, on the outskirts of Paris, he was caught in an explosion in Jack Findlay's caravan while attempting to put out a fire. Julie dragged him out but Dave died from third degree burns. Although also suffering severe burns Julie survived, and both she and her daughter Jennie have continued the great motorcycle racing tradition of the Simmonds and Boddice families. Jennie is secretary to Castrol Honda team manager Neil Tuxworth and Julie is involved with New Era club meetings around England. A quiet and unassuming person, Dave Simmonds was also a brilliant racing engineer and much of the success of the 125 was due to his developmental abilities. Dave Simmonds's life may have ended senselessly and prematurely, but he will always be remembered as being Kawasaki's first Grand Prix winner and first World Champion.

The 1966 125 racer was similar to that of 1965, with the exhausts coming from the rear of the engine. There was positive lubrication for both the main bearings and big end, and the power from the disc-valve twin was around 30–32bhp at 14,000rpm. The chassis was conventional, with a telescopic front fork, swingarm with dual shock absorbers, and a double-sided drum front brake. However, while the 1965 version was totally overwhelmed by the competition, the performance for 1966 was considerably improved.

Kawasaki's Mr Yamada offered Dave Simmonds a contract for the 1967 racing season that included a liquid-cooled 125 twin, along with a 338cc works-prepared production racer and one of the new A1R 250s. This allowed Simmonds to sell his ageing Honda 305cc twin (now in a Manx Norton frame) and concentrate on racing the Kawasakis. However, after collecting the 125 from London airport in April he found it was difficult coming in as a semi-works supported rider against the full factory Yamahas of Bill Ivy and Phil Read, let

alone the Suzukis of Yoshima Katayama and Stuart Graham. Operating out of a caravan lit by bottled gas Simmonds also struggled to overcome constant piston problems with the 125. It wasn't until a fifth at the French Grand Prix, and a fourth at the Isle of Man, that the season began to look promising. Following a third place in Finland it looked as if Simmonds had the piston problems overcome, but then he suffered a horrendous crash at the Ulster Grand Prix.

Shutting off for the fast Quarry Bends at the end of the first lap, the 125cc Kawasaki seized, throwing Simmonds off at over 100mph (160km/h). He ended up face down in a pond and only quick action from spectators prevented him from drowning. With a badly broken elbow and ankle that took a long time to heal, the 1968 season was always going to be difficult and it wasn't until the Italian Grand Prix in September that he managed a decent result (fourth). Simmonds then fronted up for 1969 with a three-year-old motorcycle, a dwindling supply of spares, and very much the under-

Simmonds on his way to victory in the 125cc Finnish Grand Prix at Imatra in 1969.

(Mick Woollett)

Although the 1967 KR-3 125cc V4 was technologically advanced most riders still preferred the twin, and development didn't proceed beyond 1968. (Cycle World)

THE 125 V4

While Kawasaki were content to provide Simmonds with only moderate support in Europe during 1967, things were different in Japan. For the Japanese 125cc series Kawasaki not only fielded a four-man team, but also produced a radical new 125cc V4, the KR-3. Their team consisted of Kanaya, Araoka, Tanaguchi and Morishita, with the KR-3 available for the Japanese Grand Prix to Kanaya and Morishita. In the race however, they both preferred the twin, finishing third and fourth.

Designed by a team headed by engineering chief Takeo Horie, the V4 began its life as a 62cc twin. The Vee was divided in a vertical line with all four exhausts exiting from the rear and the two 62cc engines were built into a box-like crankcase and geared to a central straight-cut gear. This was isolated from the crankcase chamber by seals on either side and meshed with an idler under the two crankshafts as both the cranks rotated in the same direction. Power was then taken to a 10-speed gearbox via a multi-plate dry clutch, with a water pump driven from the top of the gearbox on the right side. Ignition was by a breakerless capacitor discharge type, this being quite revolutionary for the day. The peak power was around 35bhp at 16,500rpm, but this wasn't quite enough to make it competitive against the rival Yamaha. The 100kg KR-3 had a top speed in the region of 125mph (201km/h), but during 1968 Kawasaki's priorities lay in developing the American market and moving into the more prestigious 500cc class.

dog. But even though Kawasaki had almost given up hope of winning the championship, in the wake of Yamaha officially retiring following the lead of Suzuki and MZ, Dave was quietly confident. He also felt that he had overcome the piston problems and could match his Suzuki-mounted rivals Dieter Braun and Cees van Dongen.

Although Simmonds missed the first round in Spain because the start money wouldn't cover expenses, he more than made up for this at the German Grand Prix at Hockenheim. In a pattern that would become evident throughout the season, Simmonds had trouble in practice but the bike ran perfectly in the race. Problems in practice ranged from broken crankshafts and disintegrating disc valves, to the usual piston seizures. In Germany, Simmonds gave Kawasaki their first Grand Prix victory, winning at an average speed of 96.96mph (156km/h). At the next event, the French Grand Prix, Simmonds stopped to change a spark plug, but still finished second. As both the rival Suzukis retired he went to the Isle of Man leading the championship. The Isle of Man 125 TT provided Simmonds with the first of seven consecutive victories, and he won at an average speed of 91.08mph (147km/h), with a fastest lap of 92.46mph (149km/h). In Holland he also won easily, followed by the Belgian Grand Prix at Spa Francorchamps. This race was run at an incredible average speed for a 125 of 106.89mph (172km/h) and in front of 120,000 spectators Simmonds staged an epic battle with Braun to take the race by a mere 1.7 seconds. Further victories followed in Czechoslovakia, East Germany, Finland and Italy. The title was sealed by the East German Grand Prix at Sachsenring, an event marred by the death of former 125cc World Champion Bill Ivy. In the final round in Yugoslavia at Opatija Simmons finished second to Braun after another dramatic race, giving Kawasaki the manufacturers' title. Simmonds and the Kawasaki had won eight of 11 Grands Prix, the most emphatic championship result ever in the 125cc class. Simmonds then went to Austria for a non-championship race, writing off his World Championship-winning machine by crashing into a wall. However, Kawasaki were so pleased that he had won the World Championship they provided Simmonds with a new frame and engine parts so the machine could be rebuilt.

THE A1-R AND A7-R

Soon after the release of the two-stroke 250cc A1 'Samurai' in May 1966, Kawasaki offered a racing A1-R version. Announced in December 1966, for the 1967 racing season, the rotary disc-valve 247cc (53x56mm) 180° twin-cylinder engine was similar to the street version, but for an increase in the compression ratio to 8:1. Rather than the 'Al-Fin' one-piece cylinder of the street bike, the A1-R had a pressed-in liner to provide larger ports. The two-ring pistons also had thinner (1mm) rings. There were special, 26mm Mikuni racing carburettors, with forward-mounted remote float chambers. These were designed to richen the mixture under acceleration and weaken it for braking, also reducing plug oiling. The ignition was by magneto with an external coil, and the lubrication to the crankshaft by a throttle controlled pump, supplemented by a 20:1 petroil mixture. The crankshaft was identical in design to the street version, the big-end bearings having 14 single rollers but with the NTN bearing cages being copper plated instead of silver. Inside the engine there were stronger, straight-cut primary drive gears, along with a closer ratio five-speed gearbox, and the rotary valve discs were steel rather than fibre-reinforced plastic. Apart from the clutch release there were no side engine covers and the exhaust system consisted of long, small volume expansion chambers. Along with more radical port timing these modifications provided 40bhp at 9,500rpm.

The basic chassis was also similar to the street A1 although the A1-R had a reinforced swingarm. The front forks had exposed springs without gaiters and both the front and rear brakes were upgraded. At the front was a four-leading shoe 200x20mm drum brake, with a 180x36mm drum brake on the rear. The wheels featured alloy rims, with Yokohama 2.75x18 and 3.00x18-inch tyres, these like the shock absorbers being of questionable quality. With a short (1,295mm) wheelbase and a dry weight of only 109kg the A1-R provided slightly better handling than the Yamaha TD1. It was quite a bit slower though, even if the brakes were better and it was easier to ride.

At the Isle of Man TT in 1967 Dave Simmonds finished fourth, at 92.53mph (148.9km/h), with Bill Smith fifth. Simmonds also finished fifth in the Dutch TT, and ended tenth overall in the 250cc World Championship that year. The A1-R was also successful at the Scarborough International in the hands of Swedish rider Kent Andersson, and in Australia Dick Reid won the Victorian TT at the Calder Raceway. During 1967, even before Kawasakis were sold in England, Northamptonshire enthusiast and sponsor Peter Chapman managed to import 12 A1-Rs. These had reasonable success in the hands of Chris Vincent and John Cooper.

In August 1967, Simmonds also rode a prototype A7 338cc racer to victory at Snetterton, this being basically an A1-R fitted with 62mm barrels and pistons. With the A7 already in production, for 1968 an official A7-R subsequently became available. The bore was increased to 63mm (giving 349cc), and with a 7.7:1 compression ratio, more radical valve timing and 29mm carburettors the power was 53bhp at 9,500rpm. The chassis was identical to that of the A1-R, and the A7-R achieved some success in the hands of Ken Araoka during 1968. Araoka won both the Kuala Lumpur and Singapore 350cc Grands Prix. These special versions incorporated improvements to the ignition and carburetion and would lead to the revised A1-RA for 1969.

The year 1967 also saw the modest beginning of

Dave Simmonds on the A1-R at Oulton Park late in 1968. While the brakes and handling were acceptable, the rotary valve twin was down on speed compared with the competition. (*Mick Woollett*)

the US road racing programme, Kawasaki hiring Buddy Elmore, Dick Mann and Ralph White to contest the National 250cc Road Races. However, all their A1-Rs retired at Daytona with only privateers surviving, Sonny Gager riding an A1-R to ninth. Undeterred, Kawasaki was back in 1968. Under the direction of Darryl Krause both Ralph White and Walt Fulton Jnr campaigned in the three National road races that year on A1-Rs. Future 250cc World Champion Rodney Gould also won the 250cc event at Willow Springs and this led to an expansion of racing activities for 1969, and a new A1-RA. With Ceriani-style forks and a new frame, this being an enlarged version of the double loop 'featherbed' type of the 125cc Grand Prix machine, the handling was significantly improved. The A1-RA engine featured a dry clutch with asbestos-based plates, the straight-cut primary gears being inside a magnesium cover with an outside clutch basket and release mechanism. There were larger rotary valves and 30mm Mikuni carburettors with integral float bowls and vibration-absorbing rubber mounts. Following failure of the A1-R's cast pistons at extended rpm the A1-RA had forged pistons and the big-end bearings featured a stronger cage with twin rollers in nine slots. Leading riders Cal Rayborn and Art Baumann were signed alongside Fulton and White to ride the A1-RA, with Dick Hammer an A7-R, and at Daytona all machines finished in the top ten. Rayborn was said to be extremely pleased with the Kawasaki's brakes and handling but the disc-valve twin never matched the power of the Yamaha. So, after three years campaigning the A1-R with little success Kawasaki decided to concentrate on larger racing classes in the USA from 1970.

At the end of the 1969 season, Kawasaki were ecstatic, and staged a celebration in Paris for Simmonds, this being attended by many officials from Japan. As a rule change saw the eight-speed gearbox outlawed for

1970, they also provided a six-speed gearbox for the 125, but more assistance still wasn't forthcoming. There had been no further development of the 125 in Japan, and all the jigs were destroyed. Thus, although he also received a new 500cc H1-R, Simmonds had to go it alone and, without any official financial support, was forced to race in several more profitable International British meetings early in the 1970 season. He missed four rounds at the start of the 125cc Grand Prix season, virtually handing the title to Braun on the ex-works Suzuki. Simmonds managed a second place in Holland and Belgium, a third in Czechoslovakia, a fourth in East Germany, and won in Finland. He ended the year fourth in the 125cc World Championship, but also won an important race at Brands Hatch in August. Here, he won after a race-long battle with Barry Sheene before Sheene's Suzuki broke a throttle cable.

By 1971, the 125cc Kawasaki was now too slow to be a real contender for the World Championship, and Simmonds's spare parts supply was diminishing. Undeterred, he mounted a lone challenge against Angel Nieto's Derbi and Barry Sheene's Suzuki, managing one victory, in West Germany at Hockenheim. He ended sixth in the World Championship, although he was more successful in the 500cc class on the H1-R. In 1972 Dave Simmonds again bravely campaigned the 125, now approaching six years old, as well as the 500cc H1-R. The 125 was now completely outclassed by the Derbi, Gilberto Parlotti's Morbidelli, the Yamahas of Kent Andersson and Chas Mortimer, and Borjie Jansson's Maico. Simmonds's best result was a third in the Dutch GP, along with fourth in the French, German and Spanish Grands Prix, and again he ended sixth in the championship.

With Simmonds' death at the end of 1972 so ended Kawasaki's Grand Prix challenge for several years. However, although Kawasaki took the glory for Simmonds's results, their commitment to Grand Prix racing seemed to have been dampened back in 1966 with the fatal accident of their own rider, Toshio Fujii. Simmonds's results were really attributed to his ability as a rider and engineer rather than to Kawasaki providing superior machinery. It was only when the H1-R began to achieve some success, particularly in the USA, that Kawasaki showed a renewed commitment to developing competitive racing machinery.

Below: After winning the title so easily in 1969 Simmonds struggled to be competitive during 1970. Here he is in action at the Dutch TT that year where he finished second to Dieter Braun.
(Mick Woollett)

Opposite: Simmonds bravely campaigned the ageing 125 through 1971 and 1972, but the Kawasaki was now outclassed. He also rode the H1-R and is seen here at the 1971 Dutch TT. *(Mick Woollett)*

2 AIR-COOLED RACING TRIPLES

The H1-R engine was based on the production H1 but included an outboard dry clutch and larger Mikuni carburettors. *(Cycle World)*

Although Dave Simmonds gave Kawasaki their first World Championship in 1969 and raising the company profile in Europe, Kawasaki's priority was to increase its sales in the USA. Only 3,000 large capacity motorcycles were being sold in Britain each year, yet, with about 3½ times the population, the Americans were buying 100,000 machines. With the US market in mind, September 1968 saw the release of the amazing H1, a 500cc two-stroke triple that provided astonishing performance for its price and capacity. While the H1 was successful in the showrooms, on the racetrack it proved to have deficiencies. Four modified H1s made the starting line at Daytona only weeks after the bike was available, but they all suffered teething problems. Further shortcomings became evident at both the Isle of Man and the Thruxton 500-mile Grand Prix d'Endurance for standard production machines where the H1 was totally outclassed. Not long afterwards, in December 1969, a limited production road racer, the H1-R, became available.

THE H1-R

The production H1 epitomised the Japanese motorcycles of the period in that the engine overpowered the chassis and the H1 soon earned a reputation as a fast, if somewhat ill-handling machine. Originally it had been intended to market only a racing kit for the H1 but early production racing results showed that a full racing machine would be required if the H1 was to be competitive. Thus, during 1969 the H1-R was developed in the USA, a developmental version being raced by Dave Smith at the Sears Point National. This prototype featured a Hatta-designed frame, still essentially a modified A1-RA frame (itself being based on that of the 125 Grand Prix machine), and an H1 engine developed by Yukio Otsuki. By 1970, a production series of 40 H1-Rs became available, the first in Europe going to Dutch importer Henk Vink. Most though were destined for the USA, although six also went to Australia. The H1-R was particularly significant in that they were the first 500cc racers to be offered for sale by a major manufacturer for ten years.

Forming the basis of the H1-R was a modified three-cylinder 60x58.8mm H1 engine. The five-port cylinders utilised a cast-iron sleeve with mild exhaust port timing of 194°. The transfer ports were enlarged from the H1, considerable development going into the combustion chamber with its 13mm wide squish band and shallow combustion area. The compression ratio was 7.7:1, and the two-ring pistons had 1mm rings, with the gudgeon pins offset 1mm to minimise piston slap at top and bottom dead centre. The crankshaft too was of the same forging as the street version but with additional slots in the con-rod bearing bosses for extra lubrication. As with the A1-R the 'Injectolube' forced lubrication was supplemented by petroil premix. The big-end bearings (18 rollers, with two per slot) were from the A1-RA and some early versions suffered failure where the mainshaft joined the flywheel. In the interests of serviceability the ignition was by a traditional battery, coil, and points, with conventional spark plugs. There was a five-speed gearbox, new primary drive (27/65) and the clutch was an outboard dry type similar to that of the A1-RA but with ten sintered copper friction plates. The carburetion was by rubber-mounted Mikuni VM35SC centre-float carburettors, and the power was 75bhp at 9,000rpm.

The H1-R frame featured a braced steering head, and there was a longer, square-section steel swingarm. However, the width of the H1 engine (533mm) required it to be located high in the frame to provide adequate ground clearance, with the expansion chamber exhausts crossing underneath to reduce frontal area. Another problem was the excessive thirst of the two-stoke three-cylinder engine. With an average of less than 16mpg and a five-gallon tank, the H1-R couldn't run a standard 100-mile Grand Prix. Auxiliary fuel tanks exacerbated the already high centre of gravity and the H1-R was a handful on short, tight circuits.

The telescopic forks, brakes and wheels were all specific to the H1-R, with the fork legs machined from billet aluminium and the four leading front and single leading shoe brakes laced to 18-inch aluminium rims. Although fitted with air scoops and being a generous twin 250x19mm on the front and 250x32mm on the rear, the brakes were always marginal, especially the front. Thus, while fitted to the H1-R until 1971, most were converted to a four-leading shoe Fontana or twin discs. The tyres were also marginal, these being slippery Yokohama 3.00 and 3.50x18-inch. With a wheelbase of 1,397mm and a dry weight of only 136kg, the H1-R had all the credentials to be successful. It also formed the basis of a charismatic line of three-cylinder two-stroke racing machines that provided glory for Kawasaki for the next decade. Unlike some other Japanese racing motorcycles, racing Kawasakis were produced in very limited numbers and only available to works and supported teams. Thus there were always fewer Kawasakis on the grids, but generally their distinctive green colours set them apart. The H1-R was the first of the racing Kawasakis that would be later known as the 'Green Meanies'.

Opposite: Although it looked effective the four-leading shoe-front brake was marginal and was often replaced. This restored H1-R has the 1971-style seat as developed by KMC in the USA. *(Cycle World)*

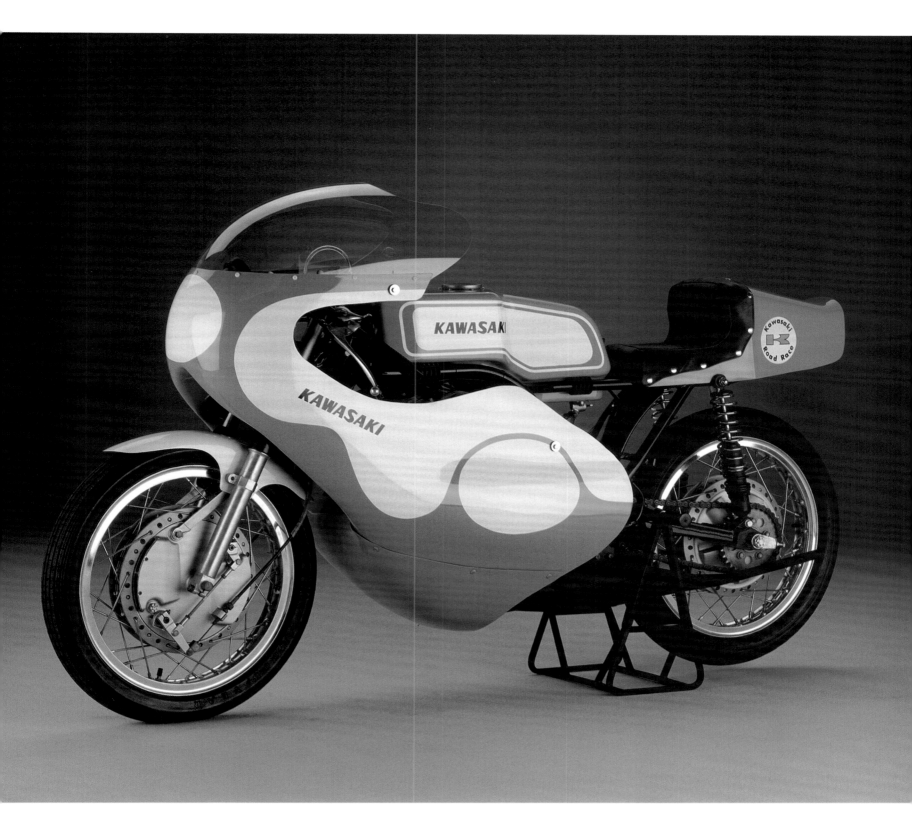

1970

The H1-R may have been a flawed machine but it made an immediate impact. In the 500cc World Championship New Zealander, Ginger Molloy replaced his 360cc Bultaco for the second round at Le Mans with an H1-R, and finished second to Agostini. Further second places at Imatra, Ulster and Montjuich saw Molloy an overall second in the 1970 500cc World Championship, albeit somewhat behind Agostini who won all but one of the 500cc races that season. However, Molloy was running a private entry, as was Christian Ravel who finished second at Spa and seventh overall. At the Isle of Man, Bill Smith took an H1-R fitted with an eight-gallon fuel tank to third in the Senior TT, the first time a two-stroke machine had been placed in the Senior in more than 40 years. While Molloy, Ravel and Smith were finding the H1-R competitive, Kawasaki's 1969 World Champion Dave Simmonds had a frustrating time with his H1-R, with continual handling and reliability problems.

Although the H1-R was surprisingly successful in Europe during its first year, it was in the USA where Kawasaki really wanted to make an impact. Rather than fielding a factory team, Kawasaki instead offered $500,000 contingency money for riders winning on Kawasakis. At Daytona, in the 200-miler, Ginger Molloy finished seventh (being timed at 159.83mph (257.17km/h) on the banking), the thirsty H1-R requiring two fuel stops. Texan Rusty Bradley took most of the contingency money, easily winning the 100-mile Amateur race on his privately entered H1-R. After Daytona the factory supplied new cylinder studs and engine mount bolts as broken cylinder studs were a problem for some H1-Rs at Daytona.

Rusty Bradley continued his winning way with victories in the Amateur Classics at Talladega, Laconia and Loudon. Dave Smith came second in the Expert event at Loudon and in Australia the H1-R also proved itself competitive. Kenny Blake rode a Ron Angel-tuned H1-R to victory in the Bathurst Unlimited event at Easter, while he retired from the 500 with a broken chain while in the lead.

Opposite: Ginger Molloy astride his new H1-R at Daytona in 1970. He finished seventh and went on to take second in the 500cc World Championship that year. *(Mick Woollett)*

Top: Through offering contingency money Kawasaki encouraged amateurs to race the H1-R in the USA during 1970. *(Cycle World)*

Bottom: Instead of running a factory team in the USA during 1970 Kawasaki left it to enthusiastic dealers to promote their image. *(Cycle World)*

THE F5-R 'BIGHORN' RACER

One of the more interesting developments by KMC during 1971 was the F5-R. For 1970 the AMA altered the rules for the Lightweight class to encourage some competition for the dominant Yamaha 250 TD2. Thus, four-stroke twins, and two-stroke and four-stroke singles to 350cc could compete against the two-stroke twins. With Kawasaki releasing their F5 'Bighorn' dirt bike during 1970, Randy Hall reasoned this engine to be suitable as the basis of a lightweight racer. The 80.5x68mm five-speed rotary valve two-stroke single displaced 346cc and was available with a speed kit barrel and piston. Randy Hall fabricated an expansion chamber, fitted a Mikuni VM35SC carburettor and a close ratio gearbox, and installed the engine in an A1-RA frame with H1-R wheels and brakes.

Mike Lane generally raced the F5-R during 1971 and it proved to have comparable speed to the Yamaha TD2, with superior handling and acceleration. The biggest weakness was the gearbox, with some of the problems being cured by fitting an F81M gearshift mechanism. At Pocono and Talladega, DuHamel also rode the machine, finishing third and fifth respectively. At the fast Talladega circuit DuHamel said that the F5-R handled so well in the infield that if the H1-R handled as well he would be 10 seconds a lap faster! For the final Lightweight event of 1971, at Ontario, a second F5-R was produced, this using a leftover H1-RAS frame, but gearbox and magneto problems saw both machines retire. DuHamel also raced the F5-R during 1972 but the team was more committed to developing the new H2-R. John Long was provided with an F5-R for the Laguna Seca Novice race, and was leading until the kickstart plug in the engine sidecover came out and dumped oil on the rear tyre.

Hurley Wilvert also built a Bighorn racer during 1971, and after he joined Team Hansen, he created another from scratch for Paul Smart. After being provided with a factory frame without engine mounts and a porous warranty crankcase Wilvert eventually managed to get the machine competitive. Smart was never happy riding the smaller racer, however, and the best result was when Nixon rode it at Ontario. Nixon was up to second before the exhaust pipe cracked, breaking in two.

Randy Hall's Bighorn singles continued to feature during 1973 and in the hands of DuHamel and Art Baumann the F5-R finally appeared to offer the potential to break the Yamaha domination at Daytona. Unfortunately, seizures in practice, and tachometer drive problems in the heat races saw them start at the back of the grid, Baumann finally finishing eighth and DuHamel ninth. DuHamel rode from last to third at Atlanta, proving the Bighorn racer was still competitive, and at Laguna Seca DuHamel led until developing engine problems, again finishing third. One of the biggest disadvantages was there were only two F5-Rs in a field of Yamahas, and despite Randy Hall's time and energy they still weren't reliable. The power though was surprising, and according to Steve Whitelock, the F5-R made 45.5bhp on the Axtell dyno. Against all odds DuHamel gave the Bighorn its best result at Charlotte in 1973, with a second place behind Kenny Roberts.

Unlike the H1-R the F5-R 'Bighorn' racer didn't fulfil its expectations. This is Hurley Wilvert at Willow Springs on the 'Bighorn' racer he built during 1971 before going to Team Hansen.

(Dennis Greene/Hurley Wilvert)

Team Hansen with their new H2-Rs at Daytona in 1972. The riders are DuHamel, Gary Nixon and Paul Smart, with Steve Whitelock, Erv Kanemoto, 'Red' Skamser, Kazuhito Yoshida, Harold Sellers, Bob Hansen, and Randy Hall. *(Bob Hansen)*

TEAM HANSEN

Bob Hansen established Team Hansen in 1953 with a team of three Indians for dirt oval racing. Later, he turned to BSA Gold Stars and when road racing started to grow in the USA successfully campaigned G50 Matchlesses. At that time he was also working for American Honda and as Honda weren't active in road racing in the States they asked him to prepare three CB450 racers for Daytona in 1967. This culminated in Hansen masterminding Dick Mann's 1970 Honda Daytona 200-miler victory. During 1970, Allen Masek of Kawasaki Motor Corporation signed Bob Hansen as the director of technical services, devoting 10 per cent of his time to the racing effort. Hansen in turn hired Randy Hall to assist with the racing programme, and Steve Whitelock and Harold Sellers as racing technicians. After the 1971 season, Kawasaki decided to have the official racing effort run outside the company, this then being taken over by Team Hansen. Bob Hansen left Kawasaki as a regular employee in November 1971. During 1972 it was reported that Kawasaki spent more than $285,000 on their 1971 road racing programme and this was undoubtedly increased for 1972. Team Hansen was very successful, with their H2-Rs winning three National road races during the year, more than any other make. This success undoubtedly prompted KMC to bring the road racing programme back to within the company for 1973, although Bob Hansen continued to manage the team. It seemed that Team Hansen was not only getting more publicity than KMC, but both KHI and KMC wanted more control over the racing programme. By the end of 1972 the riders' budget was also coming under scrutiny, as a sales slump was being predicted in the USA for 1973.

1971

Ginger Molloy left Europe to race in the USA, so it was left to Dave Simmonds to campaign the H1-R in 500cc Grands Prix. Showing typical resolve he continued to develop the machine by himself despite a hectic racing schedule. Although the factory continued to supply spares, including an H1-RA kit, he didn't get around to sorting it, and instead fitted a six-speed Fontana gearbox and had a Reynolds tubular steel frame built by Ken Sprayson. The Sprayson frame in particular was lower, stiffer, and lighter than the original and immediately Simmonds was more competitive. Unfortunately, while they did supply spares, technical assistance from the factory in Japan wasn't forthcoming. At the Dutch TT Simmonds battled with both Agostini on the MV and Rob Bron on a Suzuki before finishing third. Simmonds was runner-up at Imatra, but won the final round at Jarama in Spain giving Kawasaki their first 500cc Grand Prix victory. He ended fourth in the 500cc World Championship while Eric Offenstadt and Ron Chandler also finished in the top ten. In the 24-hour Bol d'Or race at Le Mans, Offenstadt and Charmand won the 350–500cc class, taking fifth overall, while Ken Araoka won both the Macau and Philippine Grands Prix.

Under the direction of Bob Hansen, the US racing programme was considerably expanded for 1970. The contingency money offered by Kawasaki was increased to $750,000 (for all types of motorcycle competition), this including $35,000 for the World Motorcycle Speed Record and $20,000 for a victory in the Daytona 200-miler. Not only was the contingency money increased, but KMC Racing Development supplied machines to Yvon DuHamel, Ralph White and Mike Lane. There were new H1-Rs for 1971, the H1-RA and H1-RAS, with the H1-RAS featuring new cylinders and exhausts, and a lower, lightweight frame. The H1-RAS also came standard with a steering damper, although these generally broke. The H1-RA was also slightly lighter than the H1-R, at 133kg. In January 1971, nine H1-RAs were uncrated by Team Hansen in California, some of these without forks, shock absorbers, wheels, exhaust pipes or fairings. Hansen organised Fontana brakes and Ceriani forks through Danielle Fontana and Achille Rossi in Italy, in return for H1-R spares for Giamperi Zubani (winner of the 1970 Salzburg Grand Prix). All but two of these H1-RAs ended up in the hands of privately supported experts, KMC Racing Development also having newer specification H1-RASs at their disposal.

Developments for the H1-RA over the H1-R included a Kokusan magneto CDI ignition, with a more complex advance curve, and an increase in compression to 8.0:1. Only an alternator powered the ignition, and each of the three electronic control units had six leads. Two went to a coil, three to the alternator and trigger, with the final connecting to the kill switch. With revised port timing the power was up to 80bhp at 9,500rpm, although the earlier exhaust opening at 79° ATDC often caused piston overheating. Crankshaft problems saw a redesign of the big-end bearings, now with 13 rollers (one per slot) in a silver-plated alloy steel cage. The single rollers used less oil than the dual roller type although Randy Hall doubled the oil flow to the crankshaft big-end bearing to improve crankshaft life. There were also larger fillets where the crankshaft joined the flywheel and crankshaft reliability was significantly improved. Holing pistons was more of a problem with the H1-RA engine, this seemingly being caused by the

Opposite: For 1971, there was an official Kawasaki road racing team in the USA. Here, they line up at Daytona on new H1-RAs. The riders are Ralph White (No. 47), Yvon DuHamel, and Junior Mike Lane (with the yellow plate). Standing on the right is team manager Bob Hansen, and on the left is chief mechanic Randy Hall. *(Mick Woollett)*

Right: Randy Hall weighing a piston at Daytona in March 1971. While other tuners and team members came and went, Randy Hall continued as Kawasaki's leading tuner in the USA through until the 1980s. *(Mick Woollett)*

higher compression ratio, and despite reinforcing, the crankcases often cracked. Generally, Randy Hall favoured lowering the compression ratio to 7.8:1, and piston holing was overcome after Road Atlanta through using 102 octane Union 76 racing fuel. Again, the triples' major disadvantage compared to the four-stroke opposition was fuel consumption. With the AMA limiting the fuel tank to 6.1 US gallons the H1-RA was unable to run a 100-mile race without refuelling while a 200-mile race required two stops.

At Daytona, DuHamel and Lane experienced high speed handling problems with the lightweight H1-RAS frame (nicknamed the 'lowboy'), although White tried an older H1-RA frame, modified to drop the suspension and engine one inch. C&J (Jeff Cole and Steve Jentges), a racing car frame company next door to Kawasaki R&D in Santa Ana, did this and it was more successful. The handling was also improved with the substitution of the Ceriani forks by H1-R forks. Another problem with the frame was the low swingarm pivot, contributing to excessive chain wear and the chain sometimes jumping the sprockets. In the 200-mile race none of the official machines finished. Ginger Molloy had the fastest trap speed at 155.17mph (250km/h) and was the fastest Kawasaki qualifier. Although Molloy's H1-R was extremely fast he did experience handling problems, and the rear wheel locked just after registering

During the 1971 season, H1-RA development saw a revised frame with the rear tubes connecting at a lower point to allow for a lower and more rearward fuel tank.

(Mick Woollett)

his fastest trap speed. Undoubtedly, racing an H1-R at fast tracks like Daytona required bravery, and Molloy was one of the bravest. Of the 21 Kawasakis starting the race, the best finish was Cliff Carr in 15th place, but to complete a disappointing event new Expert rider, Rusty Bradley, crashed at the first corner. Only 21 years old, he later died in hospital of severe head injuries. In the Junior race Mike Lane scorched to a 38-second lead on his H1-RAS before his lengthened gearshift lever broke.

During the 1971 season the H1-RAS was constantly developed, with the lowered C&J frame favoured over the H1-RAS item. For Atlanta there were Kawasaki forks and Girling shock absorbers and the H1-RAS engine location included two rubber mounts with a solid lower rear mount. The engine featured an H1-RAS crankshaft, cylinders and pistons with 3mm ring lands, but with earlier H1-RA cylinder heads and expansion chambers. KMC produced a new, reshaped seat, using the fairing from an H1-R, with an H1-RA belly pan.

By the time of the Kent National, DuHamel had changed to a Fontana brake, but there were traction problems. Then at Pocono there was a narrower rear wheel rim (WM2) with a harder compound Goodyear D1752 tyre, along with a 35mm shorter swingarm. One of the most effective modifications though was a lower profile aluminium fuel tank, designed to carry the fuel lower and more rearward. This also incorporated a side filler with a Bob Hansen-developed Indy-style gravity feed fuelling apparatus. Six gallons could now be dumped in only four seconds, the air coming out of the tank through a coupler at the top. It took considerable practice to perfect fast refuelling without spillage, but no one else made it work as satisfactorily as Bob Hansen. Along with the new tank came a modified frame, with the top frame rails meeting the main frame loop at a lower point. This seemingly had no detrimental affect on handling, although DuHamel was quoted as saying 'the bike shakes its head and it slides around, but there are no big problems.' DuHamel finished third after leading the first half of the race and experiencing handling and refuelling problems.

All the development on the H1-R paid off at Talladega in September when DuHamel gave Kawasaki their first US National, the 200-mile race. For this event Randy Hall reverted to H1-RAS cylinders with a 30mm high exhaust port to provide a wider powerband

than the H1-RA cylinders. However, it was a new 'soft wall' Dunlop KR83/3.50M No. 971 compound tyre mounted on a wider, WM3 rim that gave DuHamel the biggest advantage over the 750cc Triumph and BSA four-strokes. Even with two fuel stops DuHamel averaged 108.46mph (175km/h), with a top speed of around 164mph (264km/h). Ralph White finished fourth on another H1-RAS, and Mike Lane won the 100-mile Junior.

For the final National of 1971 at Ontario, California, there were new Dunlop KR83 tyres (with a No. 970 compound). DuHamel was the fastest qualifier, but with the race run in two 125-mile legs the Kawasaki team misjudged the fuel stops of Nixon's Triumph and DuHamel finished second. In the second leg oil on the track caused DuHamel to crash. However, it had been a very successful season for the H1-RA and H1-RAS, despite broken crankshafts being the most serious problem for H1-RA privateers. Over its two-year racing period in the USA the H1-R won only one National road race, but much was learned that would become incorporated in the more successful H2-R.

Yvon DuHamel at Ontario in October 1971. With its side-fill tank and new seat the H1-RA was now quite a different machine to the first H1-R. The front brake was a Fontana.

(Mick Woollett)

Dave Simmonds continued to race his Sprayson-framed H1-R in 500 Grands Prix during 1972. Here is at the start of the French Grand Prix at Clermont-Ferrand where he qualified on the front row, but failed to finish. *(Mick Woollett)*

1972

Over the winter, Dave Simmonds contacted Bob Hansen for some technical assistance, this being duly provided from Randy Hall's comprehensive racing notes. However, there was more competition in the 500 GP class during 1972, and the best result Simmonds could manage was a second in the Spanish and fourth in the German, Dutch and Swedish Grands Prix. Simmonds ended sixth overall, while Mick Grant took third place in the Isle of Man Senior TT on a Padgett-H1-R. After a mixed season in the USA Ginger Molloy took his H1-R, now with a double-disc front end from a Honda CB500, to Australia where he easily won the Victorian Senior and Unlimited TTs at Calder Park in February. Shortly afterwards he finished second in the Australian 500/Unlimited TT at Bathurst, losing by a mere 0.2 seconds.

With the KMC road racing programme now under the auspices of Team Hansen, Bob Hansen signed former Triumph stars Gary Nixon and Paul Smart to ride alongside DuHamel. Smart had impressed Hansen at Daytona the previous year, but the awaited H2-Rs were slow to materialise and during pre-season testing the Team Hansen 750s were 1971 H1-RASs fitted with tuned H2 engines. By mid-February, Team Hansen still didn't have H2-R engines from Japan and they continued testing streamlining and chassis at Willow Springs with modified street engines. These engines used reinforced production crankcases and for Daytona the bikes were basically the previous 1971 H1-RASs with strengthened frames, improved fairings, production H2 forks with double front disc brakes, and 750cc engines.

Team Hansen struggled at Daytona and Bob Hansen admitted there were handling and horsepower problems. None of the H2-Rs could break the 160mph (257km/h) barrier and factory technician Kazuhito Yoshida worked through the night to find the missing horsepower. It was all to no avail. Each of the Team Hansen machines was slightly different, reflecting the individuality of the tuners, Steve Whitelock and Harold Sellers, and there was also tension between Smart and Randy Hall. To add to the team's difficulties Cliff Carr, on a Kevin Cameron-tuned H2, was faster than any of the Team Hansen machines. Smart's race ended while on the grid, DuHamel retired on lap 14 and Nixon's gearbox broke.

Top: DuHamel on the grid at Daytona 1972 with the Team Hansen H2-R. *(Cycle World)*

Bottom: Gary Nixon on the starting line at Daytona in 1972 with his tuner, Harold Sellers. *(Cycle World)*

By the next event at Road Atlanta, engine developments centred around increasing tractability. Also by Road Atlanta, Hansen hired Hurley Wilvert as Smart's mechanic. Wilvert was also a rider, having ridden an H1-R during 1971 with Whitelock as tuner, and approached Hansen about the position as Smart's mechanic. Both Nixon and Smart still complained about the handling but when Jody Nicholas's Suzuki was disqualified for cylinder head irregularities, DuHamel inherited first place with Smart second. Smart then took his H2-R to England and had Colin Seeley build a new frame (at Smart's expense). This placed the wide engine at the lowest practical limit, and saw the engine grinding the track. Smart also took time off to win the Imola 200 (on a Ducati), and returned for the Kawasaki-sponsored Laguna Seca National with the new Seeley frame. However, because of the narrowness of the Kawasaki front forks the dual discs wouldn't fit. After reverting to the Fontana drum Smart eventually went for a single Lockheed disc with a cooling scoop to the twin-piston caliper. Later, he managed to adapt the dual Lockheed front discs. Smart was still using spoked wheels at that stage, but after Daytona, Team Hansen experimented with cast wheels. Elliot Morris was a friend of Hansen, and while many observers scoffed at the idea, Hansen commissioned Morris to build some with wider rims than they had used previously. Not only did these wheels provide wider rims, but also they overcame the problem of loosening spokes as the magnesium brake hubs expanded with the heat. The other advantage of the cast wheels was improved rigidity, and they allowed for easier fitting of disc brakes.

Apart from Smart's bike, which was noticeably improved, Nixon and DuHamel's handling woes continued at the bumpy Laguna Seca track. In the first lap of the final DuHamel crashed badly, but Smart came fourth, his hands raw from working the H2-R hard over Laguna's tight turns. For Talladega Nixon also had a Seeley frame but DuHamel won on the standard type, this time at an average speed of 110.441mph (178km/h). However, with Nixon second and Smart third the point was made and both these riders were now relatively happy with machines that had previously unnerved them. The horsepower that Randy Hall had been searching for all season came, and there was a new fairing with a larger cooler opening to reduce cylinder head temperature. Dunlop's Tony Mills also provided a softer compound KR97 tyre, the first tyre designed to cope with the higher horsepower 750cc two-strokes and heralding a new era in tyres.

Smart's day of glory came at Ontario, although it was very nearly Cliff Carr's on his Kevin Cameron-created H2-R. At the time Ontario was the world's richest ever motorcycle race, with a staggering $100,000 in prize and contingency money. In the first 125-mile heat Carr finished third, with Smart fifth, but in the second race the Kawasakis set the pace and Carr led until lap 21 when the Cameron's home-built crankshaft failed. Promised help from Kawasaki had never materialised for Cameron, and Smart cruised to victory, earning over $30,000 in prize money.

More than any other factory team, Team Hansen was committed to continual development throughout the season. This saw at least seven frame types tried, five types of cylinder, and experimentation with a wind-tunnel designed fairing. Fuel delivery problems were solved through new petcocks. Team Hansen riders also participated in several races in England during 1972, including the *Motorcycle News* Race of the Year at Mallory Park. Here, Smart won, with DuHamel second after a crash at the Hairpin. Cliff Carr too ventured wider afield, and contested the inaugural Pan Pacific Cup in Australia on his H2-R, finishing second after a win in the final race in Perth.

Along with some difficulties within the team Paul Smart struggled to come to terms with the H2-R's handling after the Triumph triple that he was used to. *(Cycle World)*

With victories in two National road races DuHamel was Team Hansen's most successful rider during 1972. Unlike the other riders, DuHamel didn't complain about the handling. *(Cycle World)*

Smart achieved more success with the H2-R after he commissioned Colin Seeley to build a frame. He raced the Seeley H2-R in England and America, this being at the Brands Hatch 'Race of the South' in October 1972. He led until forced to slow through a misfire, eventually finishing second to Peter Williams on a Norton. *(Mick Woollett)*

THE H2-R

With the 750cc H2 immediately setting the performance standard for production Superbikes for 1972, it was inevitable that a racing H2-R would follow. The AMA also decided to run the 1972 National Championship road races under FIM Formula 750 rules. By mid-1971, development of the H2-R was underway in Japan, and following the success of the KMC H1-RAS at Talladega, Mike Mizumachi of the Racing Section requested Randy Hall to despatch a frame and a fuel tank for testing on an H2-R prototype.

Despite this it was some time before the H2-R became available. When it did the crankcases differed to the production street bike although it retained the bore and stroke of 71x63mm, along with a 120° crankshaft. Development had shown weaknesses in the street crankcase and crankshaft so the crankcases now had a wider cylinder stud arrangement and extra reinforcing ribs. These were built up with weld and machined, with the engine also rubber mounted. Only 1972 models had this stud-spacing layout, and for 1973 and 1974 the H2-R used stock H2 stud spacing due to a change in Formula 750 regulations. To prevent the H1-R's occasional crankshaft breakages, the crankshaft had larger mainshafts and polished fillets where this joined the flywheel. The H2-R big-end bearing was an enlargement of the 13-roller H1-RAS design, the steel cage not only being silver plated but the rollers were also of a harder material. Unlike the street H2 the con-rods had slots, these later becoming standard on the production version, but the skinny con-rods remained a weakness. The crankshaft main bearings were roller with a machined separator to prevent high-speed cage cracking, and incorporated a machined groove and nylon insert to stop it creeping. The power was between 85 and 100bhp at 9,000rpm depending on the port timing and compression ratio. The stock compression ratio was only 6.7:1 and there was a relatively narrow power-

Above: On the left end of the H2-R crankshaft was the Kokusan CDI ignition.
(Roy Kidney)

band, from 6,500 to 9,000rpm. There was a new gearbox, high quality tool gears with coarse-pitch teeth replacing the failure-prone items of the H1-RA, and three different gearboxes available. The gearbox was trouble free, but there were problems with the selector mechanism return spring breaking through vibration, even though this had been perfect on the H1-R.

The power was fed through a new, 12-plate clutch with thinner plates, stronger springs and stronger clutch centre. From the H1-RA came the CDI Kokusan ignition, and this was problematic. The crankcase-mounted stator was vulnerable to vibration and either failed or altered the ignition timing through resistance change. While the carburettors remained at 35mm, they were a new smoothbore Mikuni. Originally developed for snowmobile use, these were designed to improve mileage while flowing the same mass. Fuel consumption remained a problem with the H2-R and, because the 750 engine drained the float chambers so quickly, the quick-fill tank needed to be spaced higher above the carburettors.

The chassis was a development of the H1-RAS, but for a dual disc front end with two 296mm discs and Tokico single-piston calipers. The rear brake was a 230x48mm drum and the standard tyre sizes a 3.00x18 and 3.30x18-inch on wire-spoked wheels. The forks were shorter than the street H2 while the general dimensions were increased slightly over the H1-R. The wheelbase was 1,382mm and the dry weight was 143kg. Despite the racing chassis it was still the engine design that limited the effectiveness of the H2-R on the track. The production H2 was designed very much as an affordable Superbike and the 750cc engine was very wide. This required the cylinders to be crowded together, limiting transfer area and ultimate horsepower. The engine also needed to be placed high in the frame for adequate ground clearance, and with the heavy engine so far from the tyre contact patches this led to oscillation on bumpy corners. Considering these design limitations the H2-R still went on to become one of the most successful of all Kawasaki's road racers, a tribute to both the tuners and the riders who campaigned them. According to Neville Doyle, who prepared H2-Rs as late as 1976, only about 35 were produced between 1972 and 1974.

1973

Throughout 1973, privateers continued to race the H1-RA in European Grands Prix, generally with a disc front end to improve the braking. Only Christian Leon and Offenstadt achieved any decent results, Leon managing fourth in the French and Offenstadt fourth in the Czech Grand Prix. For Grand Prix racing, the street-based H1-R was now too compromised, but as a Formula 750 racer the H2-R remained highly competitive.

In the USA Bob Hansen resumed management of the team, which was now back under KMC control and titled Team Kawasaki. The makeup of the team differed and Paul Smart's contract wasn't renewed. At the time this seemed surprising given his good results during 1972, but Nixon was also relegated to the status of a 'B' supported rider. The split between Smart and Hansen was probably due to influence from Japan stemming from Smart and Nixon's use of the Seeley frame, rather than a personality clash as speculated at the time. It

obviously wasn't good publicity for Kawasaki to have two of their works riders using specialist frames to overcome the poor handling of the factory H2-R. Kawasaki may have also felt that Hansen's developmental style was too independent.

The two 'A' riders for Team Kawasaki were DuHamel and Art Baumann, with Cliff Carr and Hurley Wilvert joining Nixon as 'B' riders (a term coined by Nixon). Baumann came from Suzuki with his mechanic Chris Young, while Carr brought along Kevin Cameron. Erv Kanemoto tuned Nixon's machine, Steve Whitelock DuHamel's, and Wilvert tuned his own. Kanemoto too came with considerable experience tuning Kawasakis, achieving considerable success with Walt Fulton Jnr during 1971, and Jerry Green in 1972. Bob Hansen originally wanted Wilvert to be the mechanic for DuHamel, but Wilvert approached the head of KMC R&D, Sid Saito, who agreed to Wilvert's proposal to take Paul Smart's place in the team. While this suited Wilvert it created some tension with Bob Hansen and Wilvert ended up with an H2-R created from obsolete parts.

A change to the AMA regulations for 1973 allowed more freedom in the design of frames, swingarms, wheels, brakes and fuel tanks. This was done to encourage privateers to be as innovative as the factories. A major change in race formats also saw most National road races become 75 miles (120km), eliminating fuel stops and providing closer racing. The speed bowl circuits of Daytona and Talladega now featured chicanes to limit the top speeds and emphasise acceleration. New F750 regulations required stock crankcases, cylinder castings and restricted the number of ports. Thus, with the same stud pattern and cramped cylinder arrangement as the H2, engine development was hampered for 1973. Without the room to gently curve the transfer ducts like the water-cooled Suzuki 750 it was a challenge to increase the horsepower at the same rpm while improving fuel consumption. This needed to be around 12.5mpg to complete a 75-mile race without refuelling and these design constraints led to many piston failures. To get the desired port timings the cylinders were raised on plates requiring the two piston rings to

A revised H2-R appeared for the 1973 Daytona 200-miler, but all the Team Kawasaki machines were slightly different. This has Morris magnesium wheels and heavily drilled discs. *(Mick Woollett)*

be located at the top of the forged piston to avoid the rings dropping into the inlet port at bottom dead centre. Thus there was a weakness in the lands between the piston rings, and also the gudgeon pin boss, leading to failure. Crankcase cracking under racing conditions saw new crankcases, and ball main bearings replaced the earlier rollers. Despite the limitations of the design the power was around 100bhp at 9,000rpm, some of this being due to redesigned expansion chambers that also boosted mid-range power. A firm of aerodynamic consultants in Japan designed a new fairing, with a distinctive flat area behind the front wheel.

At Daytona, Masahiro Wada joined DuHamel and Baumann as an 'A' rider, and with a factory machine and Japanese mechanics, was fastest through the speed trap, at 164.23mph (264km/h). Baumann managed to qualify second fastest but all the H2-Rs were plagued with problems in practice. These ranged from failed brake master cylinders to blown cylinder gaskets and fractured carburettor mounts. Yoshida's search for more horsepower resulted in shorter exhaust pipes and changes in compression and jetting, and the power came just in time for the race. As they had been in 1972, all the Team Kawasaki H2-Rs at Daytona in 1973 were individual creations and there was definitely a hierarchy when it came to the best equipment. No two frames were shared, and four different types of wheels were used. These ranged from wire-spoked wheels with Kawasaki discs to Morris magnesium wheels with Lockheed discs, while DuHamel resorted to the older Fontana drum brake. There were plastic or aluminium fuel tanks and either the earlier aluminium smoothbore carburettors or magnesium replicas of the H1-RA-type. These magnesium carburettors, with a 40mm bell mouth extension, provided a more progressive power delivery. Lighter brake discs were also tried, first drilled cast-iron or titanium before Kawasaki patented a process to coat aluminium with tungsten. The front forks had lighter triple clamps, and some examples had magnesium fork legs. Tyres were also critical, and although Goodyear had new slick tyres available, these looked unlikely to last the race distance so, apart from Wilvert, all were on Dunlops. After setting the initial pace, both Baumann and DuHamel crashed on the tenth lap when confronted with the debris of a fallen rider and machine. This left Nixon in the lead before

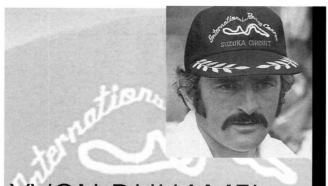

YVON DUHAMEL

Champion French Canadian rider 'Superfrog' Yvon DuHamel broke on to the US scene in a major way when he won the 1968 Daytona 250cc 100-mile classic on a Yamaha YDS-5, and finished second in the 200-miler on a 350cc Yamaha YR-2. During that period DuHamel also raced snowmobiles (for the Ski-Doo wing of Bombardier), winning the World Championship in 1970 and 1971. DuHamel's performances on the Yamaha saw him offered a lucrative contract ($30,000) with Kawasaki for 1971, and over the next few years he was Kawasaki's number one rider in the USA. Bob Hansen rated him the best Kawasaki rider of his period, DuHamel being particularly noted for his ability to ride around problems. As a non-verbal person DuHamel generally rated everything 'OK' even if the handling was diabolical. He seemed to have a super-human ability on board a motorcycle and although he had a reputation for crashing, much of this was as a result of engine failure. As Kawasaki's leading rider during the H1-R and H2-R period he was also probably responsible for Kawasaki's reluctance to accept there were any handling problems.

Born on 17 October 1939 in La Salle, Quebec, the diminutive (5ft 4in) DuHamel was also possibly the best-paid rider of the era, and his final works deal with Kawasaki (for 1975 and 1976) gave him a basic retainer of $180,000. A bad snowmobile crash over the winter of 1975–76 almost ended his road racing career and he fronted at Daytona in 1976 with a bungee cord and hook to keep his injured leg on the peg. DuHamel also rode the early KR 250, and his bilingual skills landed him some Endurance racing rides with the Godier-Genoud team. Even as late as 1982, DuHamel occasionally rode a Kawasaki Superbike in Canadian support events but ultimately the injuries sustained from a dune buggy accident saw his retirement from regular competition. DuHamel's energy then went towards promoting the successful racing careers of his sons Mario and Miguel. This even saw a return to the track in 1988, when at 48 years of age, Yvon partnered his sons on a Honda 750 in the Bol d'Or 24-hour race. They finished seventh.

One of the most fearless racers, Yvon DuHamel was Kawasaki's leading rider in the USA throughout the 1970s. He is pictured here in 1974, the year he captained the US John Player Transatlantic Trophy Team. *(Two Wheels)*

his H2-R seized (with two cracked pistons), as did Wada's. Carr and Wilvert suffered punctures so none of the factory Kawasakis finished. After Daytona, at the Dallas National, the piston cracking woes continued, sidelining all the Team Kawasaki machines except Nixon's who finished second.

DuHamel, Baumann and Carr travelled to Italy for the second Imola 200 on 15 April. With new, heavier pistons to solve the cracking problem, Baumann led initially but a crash saw him finish eighth in the first leg. Walter Villa, also on an H2-R, finished third overall with a fifth in the first race and a second in the second race. Immediately after Imola, DuHamel and Baumann, along with Nixon, went to England for the Easter John Player Transatlantic Trophy. Over three rounds between

Although a 'B' rider, Gary Nixon was the most successful rider for Team Kawasaki during 1973, winning three AMA Nationals. Here, Nixon leads at Daytona, before the engine seized. (Mick Woollett)

April 20 and 23, at Brands Hatch, Mallory Park and Oulton Park, the Team Kawasakis performed strongly, DuHamel taking one victory and being the equal top points scorer.

By Road Atlanta nearly all the factory H2-Rs were running the magnesium-bodied carburettors and squish-type cylinder heads. Although the H2-Rs were as fast as anything, and despite the best efforts of Yoshida, the troubles and seizures persisted. Two days of practice at Loudon prior to the National then paid dividends. Despite problems getting the power down out of the corners Nixon cruised home on the Kanemoto H2-R to take Kawasaki's first AMA National victory for the year.

At the second Kawasaki Superbike International at Laguna Seca, Kawasaki's bad luck of the previous year was reversed. The search for less unsprung weight saw tungsten-coated aluminium discs and, apart from Baumann, all the riders reported improved handling. In the final, DuHamel streaked away until fuel sprayed on to his rear tyre and he crashed, leaving Nixon to take his second victory in a row. Carr was second and Baumann's ignition failed just towards the end of the race. Frustration for Bob Hansen and Team Kawasaki continued at Pocono. After totally dominating the heats all but Nixon retired in the final; piston and crankshaft problems reappearing. Nixon won the race with barely enough fuel for another lap. Kanemoto experimented with Boge shock absorbers, and moved these forward to improve frame rigidity. Wilvert was running second but had one of his used cranks fail.

At Talladega, the H2-Rs were again impressively fast, but engine problems persisted. There was a new frame, which improved the handling and Dunlop provided a new, 200 compound KR97 trapezoidal round-section tyre to cope with the 175mph speeds. It looked as though DuHamel would repeat his 1971 and 1972 performances, until his engine exploded when a con-rod broke, igniting the gearbox oil and creating a spectacular blaze. At the next round, at Charlotte, DuHamel's H2-R finally kept together allowing him to take his first National victory for the year, Wilvert coming third.

The highpoint for the H2-R was the final race for 1973 at Ontario, the 250-mile Champion Spark Plug Classic run, which was in two legs. This time the piston troubles disappeared and H2-Rs took the first three places in both legs. DuHamel won both, followed by Nixon and Baumann. DuHamel's race average was 89.526mph (144km/h) in the first and 88.976mph (143km/h) in the second. Erv Kanemoto showed everyone that he could build the fastest Kawasaki as Nixon powered past DuHamel at the start/finish line lap after lap. For Bob Hansen this dominating result was the highlight of his racing career with Kawasaki. For this race Mick Grant came over from England, only to have his H2-R seize twice. H2-Rs were also raced elsewhere during 1973. DuHamel won the Canadian Grand Prix, and an H2-R was sent to Australia in February 1973, being ridden by Ron Toombs to second place in the Australian Unlimited Championship.

At Daytona in 1973, DuHamel ran wire-spoked wheels and a Fontana drum brake. There was a distinctive wind tunnel-developed fairing this year. Randy Hall is seen consulting with DuHamel on the starting line. *(Mick Woollett)*

1974

After finishing 1973 on a high point there was a considerable scaling down of the entire racing operation for 1974. With the economic difficulties imposed on KHI by the oil crisis there was a cut back in racing expenditure, and KHI knew the new Yamaha TZ750A would make life difficult for the air-cooled H2-R. There was also more emphasis on expanding racing activities outside the USA, notably in Europe and Australia, including the development of a revised H1-R for 500 Grand Prix racing. Early in the year Kawasaki announced they would be backing Christian Leon for the 500cc World Championship with DuHamel joining him for the French, Dutch and Belgian events. Both DuHamel and Leon tested this bike at Suzuka at the end of March. Developments included a six-speed gearbox, twin front discs, with the calipers cast in the fork leg, a new frame and new fairing. Although the new H1-R was totally outclassed in Grand Prix, some of these features appeared on the next generation H2-R that appeared towards the end of 1974.

Kawasaki was undoubtedly worried about maintaining their performance image in the face of the Yamaha threat, so at the AMA Competition Congress of 1973 approval was sought for a sport H2, the H2-S. This was essentially a lightweight version of the H2, with many magnesium parts and new cylinders with a divided exhaust port. Although the magnesium saved up to 7kg, it was the port divider that was most significant. This allowed the transfer ports to be raised while keeping the exhaust height the same, which also enabled a wider exhaust port without the piston rings snagging. To reduce flex in the piston there were larger gudgeon pins while new cast pistons were developed.

Within the limitations of the street H2 engine design much development was spent re-angling the transfer ports, but the stock castings of the piston-port engine still made small transfers and an early exhaust necessary. The only way to higher horsepower was to increase the revs, placing even more demand on the pistons and crankshaft. Another limitation compared with the Yamaha was the five-speed gearbox, but as this was already heavily loaded a six-speed couldn't be considered. The ultimate performance potential was always limited by the constraints of the production H2 design. This was a compromise to keep costs reasonable, with the ignition and primary drive located on the ends of the crankshaft. To keep the width to a minimum the cylinders were cast close together. Unfortunately, this limited the transfer port area, requiring even higher revs to achieve sufficient horsepower.

After being the most successful road racing team in the USA during 1973 it was surprising when KMC reduced their line-up to three riders at Daytona. Only DuHamel was retained on a full contract, but was joined by Baumann and Wilvert in lesser capacities. Randy Hall remained as DuHamel's tuner, but Bob Hansen's contract wasn't renewed. Tim Smith, racing manager of the motocross team, added the road racing team to his duties but his lack of experience led to Hall effectively running the team. Joining the KMC entries was Ron Toombs from Australia. Also evident was the general lack of development with the H2-R compared with the competition. A supplier snafu in Japan saw 300 of the newly approved A-type bridged-port cylinders being accidentally destroyed, so the bikes were much as they had been at Ontario in 1973.

Baumann came with a new mechanic, Jeff Shetler, while George Vukmanovich prepared Wilvert's H2-R,

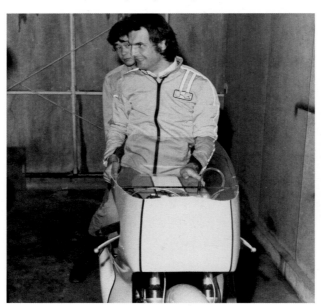

Christian Leon, with the new H1-R at Suzuka in March 1974. Also tested by DuHamel, the air-cooled 500cc triple was no longer competitive by 1974. *(Author's collection)*

this being the fastest Kawasaki at Daytona that year. Vukmanovich suggested 38mm carburettors and Wilvert used these all year. Although a Randy Hall-built frame was also available it was a development of the 1973 'Talladega' item, with a box-section steel swingarm, which was preferred. This was also a 'low-boy' type that was lighter and stiffer than previous examples. After DuHamel retired with gearbox trouble, followed by Baumann with a broken con-rod, Wilvert gave Kawasaki their best Daytona finish to date with a third behind Giacomo Agostini and Kenny Roberts. Kawasaki then hired Bob Hansen to manage the team (DuHamel and Baumann) for the Imola 200 and the Anglo/American annual Easter Match races. DuHamel captained the US team, and although he won the second race at Brands Hatch, he suffered continual engine

seizures over the rest of the weekend and couldn't repeat his performance of the previous year.

By the time of the Road Atlanta event the new divided port cylinders had arrived but they were rough cast and required detail finishing. Wilvert reverted to his older, hand-finished cylinders, and used a Harold Sellers frame, but Baumann was the highest placed Kawasaki in fourth. At Loudon, Wilvert set a sensational time to win his heat but in the final DuHamel finished fifth, his machine barely faster than Gary Scott's 750cc Harley-Davidson. Things improved at Laguna Seca, and despite badly injuring his right hand in practice, DuHamel bravely rode to second. Having his first ride on an H2-R in the US was Hurley Wilvert's protégé from Australia, Gregg Hansford, on one of Hurley's machines with a Randy Hall frame. Hansford finished fifth.

Hurley Wilvert's H2-R on the stand in the pits at Daytona 1974. There were few developments from the end of 1973, the frame featuring a box-section steel swingarm. Wilvert finished third, the best result for the air-cooled triples at Daytona. (Mick Woollett)

At Talladega the limitations of being the only air-cooled two-strokes racing in AMA Nationals were becoming apparent. DuHamel, chasing a shortfall in top speed of at least 5–10mph, crashed but Wilvert managed a sixth. Unfortunately, Wilvert crashed after the finish and broke his wrist, putting him out of action for three months. Ontario, the scene of a green wave in 1973, was even more disappointing. There, DuHamel seized yet again, but Mick Grant (on leave from Boyer Kawasaki) came a creditable seventh and Wilvert (with his left wrist in a cast), ninth. Grant was on an H2-R put together by Sacramento tuner Bob Haustien who was a friend of Bob Hansen.

In England, Stan Shenton set up Boyer Team Kawasaki with riders Mick Grant and Dave Nixon. The team was sent a 1973 specification H2-R from Japan but they had considerable trouble making it competitive. Dave Nixon was killed at the Isle of Man that year and Grant raced at selected rounds of the *MCN* Superbike Championship, finishing fifth overall. Grant also had a later specification H2-R with Morris magnesium wheels, and a box-section steel swingarm. Then at the Thruxton 400-mile 'Powerbike International' race in October, while Mick Grant was racing at Ontario, Barry Ditchburn teamed with Kork Ballington to take a surprising victory on the earlier specification Boyer H2-R. With a seven-gallon fuel tank and running street Dunlop TT100 tyres they averaged 86.33mph (139km/h) for the event. This was such a significant victory that it led to the Boyer Team receiving full factory support for 1975, and Kork Ballington was provided two of the H2-Rs. Ballington had been campaigning a Seeley-framed H2 and says, 'the works engine gave about 20 more horsepower and was a lot easier to ride. The factory bikes also handled pretty well by that stage.'

In Australia, TKA managed to obtain a new H2-R for Toombs, with Murray Sayle racing the older version. However, Toombs couldn't repeat his 1973 result, being thwarted by Gregg Hansford, leading to Hansford joining the team on an 'assisted rider' basis for 1975. At the end of 1974, Pat Hennen took Hurley Wilvert's H2-R (along with mechanic Vukmanovich) down under for the inaugural Pan Pacific series, winning the three-race series by a point from Toombs. Wilvert was still recovering from his Talladega injury.

Opposite: DuHamel on the H2-R at the John Player Grand Prix at Silverstone in August 1974. *(Mick Woollett)*

Top: Mick Grant before the start of the Formula 750 TT at the Isle of Man June 1974. Although fastest through the speed trap at 161mph (259km/h), Grant was handicapped by an arm injury and finished 17th. *(Mick Woollett)*

Bottom: Kork Ballington on his way to victory in the Thruxton 400-mile race in 1974. Ballington teamed with Barry Ditchburn on the H2-R and headed a field that included the Bol d'Or-winning Egli-Kawasaki of Godier and Genoud. *(Mick Woollett)*

1975

Later in 1974, a small number of updated H2-Rs were produced for selected teams (those not receiving KR750s) for the following season. One of these went to Australia in February 1975, initially for Toombs, but later for Hansford, and another to France for Christian Leon. While it seemed that development of the H2-R had reached a plateau in the USA, in Australia, Neville Doyle was still having some success and after Doyle procured an extra machine from Hurley Wilvert TKA had four H2-Rs at their disposal during 1975. Where Doyle seemed to succeed, where others had failed, was in the reliability. According to Doyle, 'seizures were unheard of with our H2-Rs, although a couple of times a con-rod broke at 11,000rpm.' The TKA record of 29 race wins from 31 starts during 1975, often with Hansford and Sayle in first and second places, says much for Doyle's preparation.

The revised H2-R had an engine with the newer bridged-port cylinders and featured a different frame and fuel tank. This tank was later shared with the KR750 and the new frame was similar to that of the

Gregg Hansford continued to race the H2-R successfully through until 1976. Here, Hansford and Pat Hennen battle it out at the street circuit of Gracefield in New Zealand during the 1975 Marlboro series. *(Ian Falloon)*

1975 500cc H1-RW. The wheels were Morris magnesium, the brakes aluminium with single-piston calipers, and the weight only 131kg. Consistent port development by Doyle on the H2-R saw the powerband widened from 3,000–11,000rpm. By Easter, the factory supplied one six-speed gearbox, and Doyle soon had another made as it resulted in a huge difference to lap times. At the start of the 1975 season in Australia Hansford (on an updated 1973 H2-R) was unbeatable, leading to him becoming a contracted rider from the middle of the year. When Toombs broke his arm badly in a crash at Amaroo Park near Sydney, Hansford then inherited a newer specification H2-R, finishing first in the Australian Unlimited Road Racing Championship, with Murray Sayle second. After the Australian season the team raced in the Indonesian Grand Prix at Jaya Ancol (with Abe and Wilvert), where Hansford finished fourth. He was still on the H2-R although Abe and Wada had KR750s. The team then contested the New Zealand Marlboro Series, Hansford ending second to Pat Hennen on a Suzuki 750.

The general consensus in Japan and elsewhere was that TKA had the fastest H2-Rs in the world by 1975, but as the KR750 was being raced in the USA and Europe Kawasaki in Japan didn't take TKA very seriously. Kawasaki assumed that Hansford and Sayle were winning because the competition was weak in Australia. Doyle's H2-Rs were also the most reliable. Apart from an incident with a magneto failing where the short rotor shaft sheared Doyle had no problems at all with the standard crankshafts. He maintained that crankshafts would last 2,400km, and the engines would run safely to 11,000rpm. In their second foray outside Australia TKA took their H2-Rs to the *Moto Journal* 200 in France but everything went wrong for them. Both Hansford and Sayle were also provided with factory KR750s at Ontario but the riders felt they could have gone better on their well-developed Neville Doyle H2-Rs at that stage. The high point for Hansford and the H2-R was at Bathurst, Easter 1976, where he was two seconds a lap faster on the updated specification 1974 H2-R than he was on the KR750. Neville Doyle has extremely fond memories of the final H2-R, and says, 'it was the most reliable and successful machine I ever tuned.'

TEAM KAWASAKI AUSTRALIA

In 1972, the Kawasaki distributor in Victoria, Jeff Cook, approached Neville Doyle to see if he was interested in looking after the tuning and preparation of an H2-R during 1973. The arrival of the H2-R in February 1973 then saw the establishment of Team Kawasaki Australia. With rider Ron Toombs the H2-R won 12 races from 14 starts during 1973, the only mechanical failure being caused by a chain breaking and sucking a roller into the engine. Over the next few years the TKA H2-Rs were virtually unbeatable in Australia in the hands of Murray Sayle and Gregg Hansford. Neville Doyle worked closely with the factory, continually sending engineering data back to Japan. In July 1974, all the dealers began to contribute to the team, this being matched by the factory, and in June 1975 KHI announced they would take over control of the team. This meant the team was funded by KHI, but unlike the US KMC team, it operated independently. Yet it wasn't until Easter 1976 that the factory in Japan really took any notice of TKA's achievements. 'I believe they hardly knew us,' says Neville Doyle, 'but when Hansford was faster on his older H2-R than Masahiro Wada was on the factory KR750 they couldn't believe it. We were then instructed not to race the H2-R anymore and they wanted to examine it to see why it was so fast.'

Thus began a relationship with the factory where Team Kawasaki Australia was sometimes the only official factory team. This occurred at Daytona in 1977 and in the World Formula 750 Championship during 1978. When it came to the development of the new 602S four-cylinder 750 it was to Doyle that Kawasaki turned. The close relationship between TKA and Akashi continued long after Hansford and Neville Doyle retired from racing. Neville's son Peter took over as racing manager and when Kawasaki re-entered the world of road racing in the 1990 World Superbike Championship it was Team Kawasaki Australia that received factory support.

The Team Kawasaki Australia line-up of 1975 included Gregg Hansford, tuner Neville Doyle, and Murray Sayle. Still running H2-Rs they dominated Australian Unlimited racing.
(Author's collection)

3 THE KR750

Gary Nixon at the controversial
F750 race at Venezuela in
1976. After initially being
credited victory the results
were overturned. Eventually,
the race results were annulled
and Nixon lost the
Championship. *(Mick Woollett)*

With the revised FIM homologation requirement for the FIM 750 Championship being dropped from 200 to 25 machines in October 1974, Kawasaki could finally produce a pure racing 750. Racing manager Misao Yurikusa and development chief Kazuhito Yoshida had plans for such a machine back in 1973, but this was effectively thwarted by economics and homologation requirements. As Kawasaki's racing manager since March 1972, Yurikusa was also committed to a wider programme, and one that didn't concentrate only on the USA.

As the decision to produce the KR750 (code named the 602) came after October 1974, work progressed very quickly so that the machine would be ready for Daytona in early March. Development became even more frantic when Kawasaki in Japan misinterpreted the FIM rules to indicate 25 engines rather than 25 complete motorcycles. The result was that the engines, in particular the gearbox, were initially under developed.

Central to the KR750 was a piston-port two-stroke three-cylinder engine that owed little to its predecessor. The liquid-cooled aluminium cylinders were arranged so as to provide larger transfer ports, and close cylinder spacing. The oversquare H2-R engine dimensions became square, at 68x68mm, and although the longer stroke increased piston speed, it also enlarged the port area. The pistons had a single chrome-plated 'keystone' ring. The ports were still a divided exhaust and inlet and there was not as much transfer area as expected because of the necessity to provide water jackets. The longer stroke wasn't used to provide larger transfers, and the porting was still very similar to that of the H2-R with limited room available for porting improvement. Despite liquid cooling, overheating through internal hot spots remained a problem, and it was important to keep the operating temperature below 70° C for best power.

One of the most serious problems of the H2-R, the engine width, was overcome as the crankshaft was now 19mm shorter. The pressed up crankshaft was supported by six ball main bearings, these now being all the same size and without smaller timing side bearings like the street H2. Despite the longer stroke the con-rods and big-ends were identical to those of the H2-R and forced lubrication through three of the main bearings fed to the respective crankpins. The primary drive was by straight-cut gears with a 1.89:1 reduction, with the primary gears also driving the water and oil pumps. The factory guaranteed the crank, pistons and small ends as being good for 1,300km, the cylinders for 5,000km, and the cylinder heads for 8,000km. Neville Doyle claims he never had a crank apart and simply replaced the complete unit after 1,600 racing kilometres, but it was important they were true. Others, like Team Boyer Kawasaki in Britain sometimes found crankshaft life to be as little as 100km. With Mikuni 35mm carburettors the power was around 120bhp at 9,500rpm, but came in strongly at 6,500rpm giving a much narrower powerband than the final H2-R.

Outside the engine was a wide, 24-plate steel dry clutch and inside the wider gearcase was a six-speed gearbox. There were some initial problems with the design of the gearshift and shifting shaft that was increased to 13mm (from 12mm) following failure on the H2-R. The chassis included hand-built Kawasaki forks, Koni shock absorbers and Morris magnesium wheels. The brake discs were the usual steel-coated aluminium (296mm on the front and 232mm on the rear). All this was packaged in a lighter and better handling chassis than the H2-R, the dry weight being around 147kg. The frame (constructed from 28mm tubing) featured an updated rubber engine mounting system, more bracing around the steering head, and a 27° fork rake. With a box-section swingarm constructed of thin-wall tubing and 18-gauge sheet steel, the frame

Top: The liquid-cooled three-cylinder KR750 engine owed little to its air-cooled predecessor, but was arguably out-of-date even before it was produced. *(Two Wheels)*

Bottom: The widest part of the KR750 engine was the outboard multi-plate dry clutch. This is Gregg Hansford's KR750 from 1976; early machines like this having a smaller radiator. There were 38mm Mikuni carburettors for 1976. *(Two Wheels)*

Another view of Hansford's 1976 KR750. The vertical shock absorbers were Mulholland and the rear Goodyear slick tyre a 3.50x18-inch. The 22mm rear disc was metal-sprayed aluminium.
(Two Wheels)

The Team Boyer Kawasaki machinery in their Bromley workshop in early 1975. In the front on the left is an H1-RW, with two KR250s.

(Two Wheels)

TEAM BOYER KAWASAKI

It wasn't until the formation of the wholly owned subsidiary Kawasaki Motors (UK) Limited in 1974 that Kawasaki seriously considered supporting racing in Britain. Due to the oil crisis this was during a period of uncertainty and there had already been a severe cutback in racing activities in the USA. With this in mind the British directors, Michio Uchida and John Norman, approached Stan Shenton regarding the establishment of an official racing team. Shenton provided the required specialised knowledge and experience, as well as all the contacts in the racing business.

Coming from a family that had held a Triumph motorcycle franchise since 1927, Stan Shenton took on the Kawasaki contract after nearly 20 years in the motorcycle trade. Prior to this he had been in the Royal Air Force and a Lloyds insurance broker. Shenton's Bromley business sponsored the successful Boyer-Triumph team and as Team Boyer Kawasaki their first efforts were tentative. Mick

Grant was signed as the lead rider to compete in selected 1974 events. After victory in the Thruxton 400-mile race later in the year KHI, and particularly Yurikusa, were so pleased that Team Boyer Kawasaki received full factory support for 1975. This included four KR750s, five KR250s, and two H1-RWs. Ken Suzuki, formerly of Tohatsu and Bridgestone, joined the team to liaise directly with the factory. The British KR750s came with rough cast unported cylinders, these being finished by Team Boyer mechanic Nigel Everett. The aluminium brakes were changed to stainless steel and Girling shock absorbers were fitted. Despite the team's 1975 success a general cutback for 1976 almost saw an end to the British racing programme until increased financial support came from Hodge Finance Ltd. There was then less concentration on World Championship events but even when the racing Kawasaki effort moved away from the Boyer team the Shenton influence remained with Stan's son Stuart as one of Ballington's mechanics.

DuHamel on the new KR750 at Daytona in March 1975. This first outing was inauspicious and all five KR750s retired.
(Two Wheels)

weighed 10kg. The brakes and handling were excellent and it was more than a match for the twin shock absorber Yamaha. Even when the Yamaha TZ750 adopted a monoshock rear suspension system the KR750 was often able to match it in acceleration because of its lighter weight.

After the devastation of 1974, 21-year-old Jim Evans joined DuHamel Team Kawasaki in the USA for 1975. Shetler looked after Evans's machines while, as usual, Randy Hall prepared DuHamel's. For Daytona, also the first round of the FIM 750 Championship, there were five riders on KR750s. Mick Grant and Barry Ditchburn came over from England two weeks before the race, and were joined by Takao Abe from Japan. However, success at Daytona doesn't come easily, and the KR750s were not only new but also slow. The Yamaha TZ750 was now a full 750cc and it was back to the old business of cutting pistons and porting cylinders trackside

for Kawasaki's mechanics. All the KR750s had gear selection problems and modified clusters were flown out from Japan. The KR750s were also slightly different, Abe's being the fastest and also the fastest Kawasaki qualifier. In the feature race gearbox and crankshaft problems saw an end to all the KR750s, although Ditchburn, with the slowest machine, lasted the longest.

At the second round at Imola, again the KR750s were stricken with problems. DuHamel suffered over-heating, Jim Evans holed a piston, and Ditchburn crashed. The only Kawasaki to finish was Grant with a fifth in the first leg, but a hasty strip down between races to check a piston robbed him of a second leg ride. Returning to Britain immediately after Imola, Team Boyer Kawasaki began developing their KR750s and made an outstanding start in the British *Motor Cycle News* Superbike Championship. Development included revised porting, carburettors and exhausts, and at the opening round at Cadwell Park Grant won easily, Ditchburn falling while in second place. Grant then repeated this victory at Brands Hatch, Ditchburn coming second. As there were no Yamaha TZ750s in the British Championship in 1975 this undoubtedly aided Grant and Ditchburn, Barry Sheene's Suzuki 750 providing the only real competition.

The Isle of Man TT of 1975 provided Kawasaki with one of their more memorable achievements. Although Ditchburn was never happy on the island circuit, Grant was a road circuit specialist. He had already won both the 750 and 500cc races at the North-West 200, setting a new outright lap record of 122.62mph (197.3km/h), and at the Isle of Man not only won the Senior TT (on the H1-RW) but also broke Mike Hailwood's long-standing outright lap record. This occurred in the Open Classic TT where he lapped at 109.82mph (176.7km/h) before breaking a chain. Ditchburn may have disliked the Isle of Man but he made up for it at the annual post-TT Mallory Park

meeting. Here, Ditchburn rode one of the best races of his career to beat Barry Sheene and set a new outright lap record at 97.98mph (157.65km/h).

After Mallory, the team travelled to Mettet in Belgium for round three of the FIM 750 Championship and Grant immediately set the pace until his machine seized at a 140mph (225km/h) left hander. Although his boot was ripped off, somehow he managed to stay on. Ditchburn then looked certain to win until he ran out of fuel just before the end. Team Boyer Kawasaki were balancing the FIM 750 Championship events with the British Championship so at the French 750 round at Magny Cours a week later DuHamel upheld the Kawasaki flag, but his KR750 seized in the first leg.

In the British Championship the absence of Barry Sheene allowed Grant to take the victory at Scarborough. A second place at Mallory Park then saw him leading the Championship and Ditchburn sealed it for Kawasaki by winning the final race at Brands Hatch, also setting a new lap record. He finished second in the *MCN* Superbike Championship behind Grant. It had been a spectacular debut season in Britain for the KR750, but it wasn't only in the Superbike Championship that the Kawasakis impressed. Where possible, Team Boyer Kawasaki also competed in other rounds of the FIM 750 Championship. At Anderstorp, staged in conjunction with the Swedish Grand Prix, Ditchburn won the second leg and came second overall, while Grant retired with yet another crankshaft failure. This was the first time Ditchburn had used a Dunlop slick front tyre and he found the KR750 much improved. At the 750cc John Player British

Barry Ditchburn leads Barry Sheene at the F750 race in Anderstorp in 1975. The Dunlop slick front tyre can be seen here. Sheene was on a treaded Michelin, and Ditchburn won.
(Barry Ditchburn)

Grand Prix Ditchburn rode to a second place behind Sheene in the second leg, also setting a new lap record at 112.10mph (180.37km/h). Ditchburn also won the 'King of Brands' title at Brands Hatch. DuHamel won both legs at the Dutch FIM 750 Championship round at Assen, giving the KR750 its first victory in the championship. Here, Ditchburn again impressed by setting equal fastest lap but retired with engine problems.

In the USA, there were only two more road races after Daytona as the Atlanta event in June was cancelled. This gave Randy Hall some time to develop the KR750. He flew to Japan to create a new set of exhaust pipes and with the problems of gearbox failure and overheating largely overcome, further testing at Laguna Seca saw the KR750 running strongly. Hall also developed an experimental linkage parallelogram swingarm. This became known as the FUBAR (an old US Army term standing for 'Fouled Up Beyond All Repair') and provided anti-dive and anti-squat. It had also been in development for some time, being tried earlier on an H2-R and also by Jim Evans at pre-Daytona testing. DuHamel practised on the KR750 FUBAR at Laguna Seca but the contorted exhaust system robbed power, so he raced the regular KR750.

At Laguna Seca in August, the KR750 finally emerged as a serious threat to the Yamaha domination when DuHamel trailed Kenny Roberts across the finish line in the heat race. DuHamel was running regular (rather than the newest type) Goodyear slick tyres and was comfortably leading Roberts until he crashed at the corkscrew, the scene of his crashes in 1972 and 1974. This time though the culprit was an outer crankshaft bearing cage that had disintegrated tearing an outer oil seal that allowed crankcase pressure to blow gearbox oil out the breather and on to the tyre. At Ontario Kawasaki had an extremely strong team including DuHamel and Takao Abe riding FUBARs (now with revised exhausts), Grant and Ditchburn from England, Wada from Japan, and Gregg Hansford and Murray Sayle from Australia. DuHamel managed third overall with a seventh in the first leg and second in the second leg, showing the new chassis' potential. This race was to be the last for factory Kawasaki triples in the USA, as for 1976, racing would be through 'supported dealers.'

MICK GRANT

With his win in the 1975 *MCN* Superbike Championship, Yorkshireman Mick Grant gave Kawasaki a huge boost in Britain. Born on 10 July 1944, Grant came to Kawasaki after his first Isle of Man TT victory, in 1974. That year, on the legendary 'Slippery Sam' racing Triumph Trident, he won the Production TT. It was only by accident that Grant took up road racing. During 1967 he was competing in motocross on a Cotton 250cc Scrambler but as he was riding a Velocette Venom on the road decided to try his hand at road racing. While moderately successful in club events, Grant's lucky break came in 1970 when he teamed up with Jim Lee, a manufacturer of racing equipment near Leeds. That year Grant won 16 races on Lee's BSA Gold Star. The association led to the distinctive 'JL' initials on his helmet, remaining long after their racing relationship ended at the end of 1971. In 1972, Grant won the British 350cc Championship on a Padgett Yamaha, also coming third in the Junior and Senior TTs that year. As a professional privateer he was signed by the John Player Norton Team for 1972 and 1973. Grant notched up Norton's first Superbike win in England at Scarborough, also coming second in the 1973 Formula 750 race at the Isle of Man, but despite these results he was eased out of Norton's line-up.

His TT exploits and Superbike results in 1975 saw his popularity soar and during the later 1970s Grant was one of the most popular riders in Britain. At the end of 1976 he held a total of ten 750 and outright lap records at British circuits and Grant was one of the first riders to appreciate the importance of a good liaison with the press. After a disappointing season with Kawasaki in 1978, he was signed by Honda to ride Formula One and develop the four-stroke NR500 for 1979. Grant crashed the NR500 on the first corner in the British Grand Prix, but won the 1980 TT Formula 1 Championship, continuing to race successfully through until 1985 when he took out the British Superstock Championship on a Suzuki. He then retired from racing, one of the few riders of the era to manage to make a respectable living from racing motorcycles. As a Kawasaki rider it was his feats on the KR750 that have been most remembered, especially at the Isle of Man, but Grant also gave the KR250 its first Grand Prix victory. In the words of a competitor, 'he achieved his results by being extremely tenacious and really worked hard at it.' Grant was also clever, not only managing to sustain a career over 15 years, but also securing contracts with four different factory teams, three of them Japanese.

Always one of the most popular riders, Mick Grant gave Kawasaki some of their most significant victories in Britain. For several years the names of Grant and Kawasaki were synonymous. *(Author's collection)*

THE H1-RW

Opposite: Mick Grant awaiting the start of the 1975 Senior TT at the Isle of Man. Grant rode the H1-RW to victory while Charlie Williams on the Yamaha next to him was seventh. The H1-RW no longer had the brake calipers cast with the fork leg.
(Mick Woollett)

Right: Soon after his victory at the Isle of Man, Grant rode the H1-RW in the 1975 Dutch TT at Assen. There were new front brake calipers but generally the performance and reliability of H1-RW was disappointing in Grands Prix.
(Mick Woollett)

The career highlight for the liquid-cooled H1-RW was Mick Grant's victory in the Senior TT at the Isle of Man in 1975. For this race the Kawasaki factory sent out a new machine after Stan Shenton had promised them they would win the Senior. Fortunately, Shenton had faith in Grant's abilities and rewarded Kawasaki with their first 500cc Grand Prix victory since 1971. Only a month before, Grant had taken the new H1-RW to victory in the 500cc race at the North-West 200 at an average speed of 116.06mph (186.74km/h), with a fastest lap of 117.49mph (189.04km/h), so it was no surprise to see him dominate at the Island. Ditchburn also had an H1-RW for the TT but was never as comfortable on the fast street circuit. Despite losing power through a partial engine seizure, Grant easily won the six-lap race as there was little competition, his fastest lap being only 102.905mph (165.61km/h).

After the Isle of Man TT, Grant, Ditchburn and DuHamel rode H1-RWs at Assen in the Dutch TT. All the 500cc Kawasakis retired. After qualifying eighth, Grant only lasted seven laps in Belgium before a piston holed, and at Sweden Ditchburn looked like passing Phil Read on the MV to take second but was halted when the ignition unit dropped off the drive shaft and breaking the crankshaft. Grant was up to third before his H1-RW broke a gearbox. This was to be the final Grand Prix for the H1-RW, although there were some more outings in England. At the 1976 Hutchinson 100 at Brands Hatch Ditchburn and Grant were third and fourth in the 500cc race. According to Barry Ditchburn, 'the 500 was a lovely bike to ride, but simply wasn't powerful enough. It could match the four-stroke MV but that was about it.'

Weighing around 136kg and producing 88bhp at 9,500rpm, the H1-RW was neither light nor powerful enough to beat the four-cylinder Grand Prix Yamaha and Suzuki. Although it steered and handled well the mechanics claimed it was difficult to work on. The H1-RW was also unreliable, the weight of the generator on the end of the crankshaft contributing to premature crankshaft failure.

1976

Initially there was to be no official road racing operation in the USA for 1976, with semi-works support going exclusively to Gary Nixon and Ron Pierce. A change of heart at the last minute though saw Yvon DuHamel back with a works contract, his KR750 again being wrenched by Randy Hall. DuHamel had the FUBAR KR750, but early in the season he was still recovering from a broken leg. Thus Pierce had to test his bike, promptly crashing it. Gary Nixon and tuner Erv Kanemoto were supplied a 1975 KR750, and after his efforts with the development of the KR250 during 1975 Ron Pierce also received a KR750. Pierce brought his previous year's TZ750 tuner, Kevin Cameron.

At Daytona, Tim Smith managed the US team, which was joined by Team Kawasaki Australia rider Gregg Hansford with a new KR750 tuned by Neville Doyle. Contract complications saw Shenton's team remain in England. Hansford received his KR750 in January and immediately won the Australian Unlimited TT at Laverton, beating Suzuki-mounted Pat Hennen after a monumental dice. The 1976 KR750 had a different fairing and forward-mounted twin-piston front brake calipers. There were new crankshafts, presumably safe to 10,000rpm, stronger con-rods with a larger big-end eye, and new crankcases with grooves to clear these thicker big-ends. Generally though, the new cranks still proved unreliable. Carburetion was now by 38mm Mikunis, although the peak power was unchanged, and the dry weight was 143kg.

Small problems dogged the KR750s all week at Daytona. The forks were bending under load and there were handling problems. On top of that pistons were melting and the top speed was considerably down on that of the new Yamaha TZ750A. However, in the 200-miler the leading Yamahas had tyre problems and the KR750s gradually worked their way up the field. Hansford was in third until his chain broke, and Nixon ended second. It was to be the KR750's best result at Daytona.

After Daytona the FIM 750 Championship continued at San Carlos in Venezuela, a meeting dogged by controversy. Nixon's crank failed in practice, also destroying the crankcases, and he borrowed an engine from Neville Doyle. In the first leg, Hansford's KR750 overheated, and Nixon was credited with second after Steve Baker had pulled into the pits on the second lap to adjust a carburettor. Baker won the second leg, with Nixon second, the timekeepers confirming Nixon's victory, but four hours later this was overturned and Baker was credited with the win. It would take until the FIM Congress in Belgium in October for the confusion to be settled.

Bad luck continued to dog Nixon when his KR750 was lost in transit. Initially it was thought to have been sent to Australia by mistake and it didn't turn up until the Match Races in England over Easter. At Imola, DuHamel was the best-placed Kawasaki, in seventh, while both Ditchburn and Grant's 'new' crankshafts expired. Most of the leading competitors boycotted the Spanish event due to a lack of starting money, but the KR750s were back in force for the next round at Nivelles in Belgium. Grant and Ditchburn promptly set the pace but Nixon surprised everyone by winning the first leg after Ditchburn's engine seized while in the lead. Ditchburn though had the fastest lap at 99.764mph. In the second leg Nixon finished second to Grant, taking the overall victory. A week later, at Nogaro in France, Nixon kept his Formula 750 title hopes alive with a fourth overall, while both Ditchburn and Grant crashed.

Nixon then went back to the USA for the Loudon National and there Kawasaki provided support for him, along with Pierce and DuHamel. At a circuit where he always excelled, Nixon was leading the field comfortably until he crashed inexplicably. DuHamel came sixth. As he had during 1974 for Nixon's Suzuki, Kanemoto commissioned a replacement frame from C&J in Santa Ana for the KR750. This was expected by Loudon but it was not available until Laguna Seca. Looking similar to the standard item, the C&J-built frame used larger diameter tubing (35mm) and a steering head fabricated from 3mm alloy plate, although it looked as if it was machined from a solid billet. The engine was also mounted slightly lower and as far forward as possible. Early testing found the swingarm too short, but even with a longer swingarm the wheelbase was still slightly less than the standard KR750, at around 1,397mm. The rear suspension was conventional, with twin laydown Mulholland shock absorbers. The brakes were Fontana and Nixon immediately preferred the new chassis over the standard item.

At Laguna Seca Nixon's new chassis and his Michelin tyres worked well enough to give him second in the first 100km leg. He was also third in the second leg before he crashed. Only DuHamel on the FUBAR finished both legs, but only for seventh overall. After Laguna, Nixon and Kanemoto took the KR750 to Silverstone where Grant had pole position but retired with a broken chain. Nixon's crankshaft failed after 29 laps in the first leg and an argument over appearance money saw him refuse to fit another engine for the second leg. In retrospect this was a flawed decision as it allowed Palomo to gain vital championship points. The next round at Assen was miserable for Nixon as he got caught on slick tyres after it started raining, ending 17th. A snapped gear selector shaft in the second leg saw him with no points and the championship slipping away. For this round, Ditchburn was representing Kawasaki UK and had a new crankshaft, presumably raising the safe rev limit from 9,000rpm to 10,000rpm. Grant remained in England in an endeavour to win his second British Superbike Championship.

Both Ditchburn and Grant also journeyed to the final round at Hockenheim, Ditchburn achieving pole position. A refuelling problem in the first leg saw Nixon

lose time and he finished seventh, just behind Ditchburn. Grant missed the start of the second race, but Nixon held on to win and take second overall. Both Nixon and Palomo claimed the championship so it came down to the FIM Congress, but a final decision couldn't be made so the Venezuelan results were deleted, robbing Nixon of the victory that he deserved. If they had been included Nixon would have won. It had been a frustrating season for the semi-official rider as factory assistance wasn't forthcoming and he lacked sponsorship. Racing a KR750 was considerably more difficult than a comparable Yamaha or Suzuki because racing parts were unique to the racing department and not shared with any street model. Considering the level of competition Nixon's result was extraordinary, and a tribute both to him and Kanemoto.

Back in the USA, Pierce finished fifth at Riverside, with Nixon and DuHamel rounding out the top ten. Here, even after having the most successful KR750 in Europe, Kanemoto struggled to get a new crankshaft. By this stage it was obvious that Kawasaki were no longer enthusiastic about pursuing 750cc racing seriously in the USA.

As the Boyer Team Kawasaki were so successful in Britain during 1975, Kawasaki expected them to do even better during 1976. There were still no official Yamahas racing in Britain so their only competition came from Barry Sheene's Suzuki. However, early in the season the Kawasakis suffered from persistent crankshaft problems and engine seizure. Rechamfering the exhaust bridges solved the seizure problem and at the annual Easter Transatlantic Trophy Ditchburn and Grant finished every race. Without the benefit of the latest engine parts from Japan the British team worked on the handling, and had Girling produce new gas-pressurized shock absorbers.

It wasn't until Brands Hatch in May that the 'Green Meanies' won their first race in the British Superbike Championship. Grant led from start to finish with Ditchburn second. Even though Grant was the first rider to pass the 110mph barrier in practice, the Isle of Man was dismal after the success of the previous year. At the post-TT Mallory Park meeting Grant crashed, although Ditchburn came second. Then at Silverstone, in support races for the British Grand Prix, the Kawasakis returned to form when Grant won the second leg of the Formula 750 race. The previous day he

Although Mick Grant didn't win at the Isle of Man in 1976, in practice on the KR750 he was the first rider to lap at more than 110mph (177km/h). *(Two Wheels)*

The closest the KR750 came to winning at Daytona was in 1976 when Nixon came second on his Kanemoto-tuned machine. Here, he leads the Suzuki of Barry Sheene. *(Two Wheels)*

GARY NIXON

When Gary Nixon came second in the FIM 750 Championship he was already a seasoned veteran. Always noted for his slight build, Nixon was born in Anadarko, Oklahoma on 25 January 1941. At the age of 15 he began racing in off-road events in Oklahoma City on a Triumph 650. Turning professional in 1958, he became an officially sponsored rider for Triumph from 1964, also riding Yamahas in the smaller categories. Against the might of Harley-Davidson he was 1967 and 1968 AMA Grand National Champion, on a Triumph, riding the final 1967 National with a broken thumb. In 1968 he was also the first rider to win the 200-mile and 100-mile Lightweight races at Daytona in the same year. A terrible accident during 1969 almost saw his left leg being amputated but he recovered to race through 1970 before breaking his thigh at the end of the year. Dropped by Triumph at the end of 1971, Nixon signed for Team Hansen in 1972, but for 1973 was demoted to the status of a 'B' rider. That year saw the beginning of his relationship with Erv Kanemoto and it was one of Nixon's most memorable with three AMA National Road Race victories.

Californian-based Kanemoto was born in Utah in 1942 and started tuning outboard engines before progressing to go-karts in 1958. He became committed to motorcycles after spending a season tuning Walt Fulton's H1-R in 1971. Expecting to remain with Kawasaki during 1974, the surprise cut back in KMC's racing expenditure saw Nixon and Kanemoto with Suzuki, but only after MV Agusta had made an offer. Both 1974 and 1975 were seasons to forget for Nixon as he crashed badly in June 1974 and then spent most of 1975 recovering from injuries sustained at Daytona and testing an RG500 Suzuki in Japan. A determined and tough rider, the 5ft 4in Nixon was the closest he came to winning a World Championship in 1976. Nixon and Kanemoto then left the Kawasaki camp and campaigned a Yamaha TZ750 through until 1978. Many years later Nixon was still racing at Daytona, winning the Legends races overall in 1995. Gary Nixon represented another era of motorcycle racer. When asked to comment on his lifting the back wheel three inches under hard braking at Loudon in 1976 Nixon replied, 'I never knew that was happening, until someone showed me a photograph.'

finished a close second to on-form Steve Baker on the Bob Work Yamaha OW31 proving that on its day, and in the right hands, the KR750 was still a force to be reckoned with. Both Baker and Grant shared the fastest lap at 113.79mph, a new outright record.

Such a performance was undoubtedly a boost for the next Superbike round at Oulton Park where Grant and Ditchburn again finished first and second. With Ditchburn in Assen, Grant won the next round at Oliver's Mount at Scarborough, but Sheene (on an oversized RG500 Grand Prix machine) defeated the Kawasakis at the final three rounds at Mallory Park, Cadwell Park and Brands Hatch. This gave Sheene the Championship ahead of Grant and Ditchburn. In other British International meetings that year Grant and Ditchburn continued to provide Kawasaki with good results. Grant won at Cadwell Park in May and the Race of Aces at Snetterton in July, while Ditchburn won the Powerbike race at the Race of the South meeting at Brands Hatch.

In Australia, Team Kawasaki Australia continued their winning way, but with Hansford also competing in selected international events he was unable to win the Australian Unlimited Championship. With one KR750 supplied, Sayle continued with the H2-R, but at Bathurst Masahiro Wada came out from Japan with a factory KR750. Wada came third and this was the event that Hansford impressed on the older, air-cooled bike. TKA won 21 races from 27 starts in Australia that year, but their decision to compete in the Indonesian Grand Prix cost Hansford the Australian Championship. However, as he finished second at Indonesia this undoubtedly contributed to the elevated status of TKA for 1977.

Unlike Erv Kanemoto, Neville Doyle was happy with the standard frame, instead concentrating on suspension development. He favoured softer suspension with more controlled damping, and there were new damper rods for the forks with changes to the compression and rebound damping. This saw an increase in the fork travel by 55mm, to 115mm, and softer, progressive 40/60lb springs. At the rear Doyle also modified the twin Boge Mulholland shock absorbers, these also having softer (60/90lb) springs. Wada rode with Hansford's suspension at Bathurst, immediately lowering his lap time by four seconds.

1977

For the 1977 season there was a new model KR750, this the lighter 602L. With no official US road racing by KMC for 1977 Team Kawasaki Australia represented the factory at Daytona. Neville Doyle prepared new 602Ls for Gregg Hansford and Murray Sayle. The 602L was the final version of the KR750 and weight reduction extended to magnesium crankcases and an aluminium clutch. The dry weight was now 136kg and other developments included a larger radiator to overcome earlier cooling problems, and a new ignition system that fired all three cylinders simultaneously, 120° apart. The cylinders now had an unbridged exhaust port along with four transfer ports. To isolate the 38mm carburettors from vibration these were mounted on the chassis and connected to the inlet ports with soft rubber boots. There were new rear-mounted brake calipers and a combined front wheel bearing and disc mounting. The rear axle was now held in eccentric adjusters, a cantilever brace stabilised the swingarm, and the shock absorbers more layed down. Even with this development the 602L was initially outclassed by the Yamaha TZ750, and at Daytona Hansford was considerably down on speed. Where he was superior though was in braking and after a truly impressive display of riding finished fourth in the rain-shortened race. A week later at Charlotte Hansford managed third after a race-long duel with Gene Romero.

Team Kawasaki in the UK also received new 602Ls and Ditchburn gave them their first victory in the non-championship Formula 750 race at Nogaro in France in March. The British team then joined Hansford at Imola for the second round of the FIM Formula 750 Championship where Hansford finished sixth in the first leg, the only Kawasaki to figure in the results. At the annual Transatlantic Trophy Match races Grant and Ditchburn (along with Phil Read on a 1976 KR750) were the only Kawasakis competing. Despite being down on speed the two new 602Ls finished every race, Grant coming second in the second leg at Oulton Park.

Generally though the 602L wasn't as successful as Kawasaki had anticipated. Hansford didn't compete in

Opposite: Team Kawasaki Australia finally received a KR750 for 1976, Gregg Hansford again proving virtually unbeatable in Australia. Hansford generally raced with the number '02' in Australian races. *(Two Wheels)*

This page, top: To isolate the Mikuni carburettors from engine vibration these were frame-mounted on the 602L. *(Roy Kidney)*

Middle: By the end of 1977 Gregg Hansford and Neville Doyle had the 602L performing magnificently. Here, Hansford checks his machine at Laguna Seca where he finished third overall. *(Cycle World)*

Bottom: Yvon DuHamel generally raced with the number '17' and achieved respectable results on the 602L as late as 1978. *(Roy Kidney)*

Opposite: There was also a number of chassis developments, including a braced swingarm with eccentric axle adjusters. *(Roy Kidney)*

the Formula 750 race in Spain, and although Grant and Ditchburn qualified third and fourth, Grant ran off the circuit and Ditchburn's engine expired. At this stage in the season Hansford concentrated on the Australian Unlimited Championship, which he won. Rick Perry came second and Murray Sayle third, both also being KR750-mounted.

The British team didn't race at the Dijon-Prenois round of the 750 World Championship due to insufficient start money and also made a disappointing start in the *Motor Cycle News* Superbike Championship. Grant and Ditchburn both struggled for results with Grant's best performances again being at the North-West 200 and the Isle of Man. At Ulster he won the Superbike race at 119.692mph (192.625km/h) and at the Isle of Man Grant again set a new outright lap record of 112.776mph (181.496km/h) on his way to winning the Classic TT at an average speed of 110.768mph (178.264km/h). After this race Kawasaki's fortunes in the Superbike Championship improved, although it wasn't until Scarborough in September that Grant won a round. He then won the final race at Brands Hatch to end up second overall yet again.

At the British Formula 750 round at Brands Hatch in July Grant hounded Steve Baker all the way in the first leg, failing to win by only 2½ seconds. Although Grant crashed in the second leg, Ditchburn recovered from earlier brake problems to finish third. There was then no Kawasaki representation in the 750 World Championship until Laguna Seca in September. Returning to the USA Hansford again demonstrated his and Neville Doyle's outstanding capability. Their 602L was now a world-class road racer and Hansford, with a second in the first heat and third in the second, came third overall. A week later at Mosport Park in Canada, DuHamel joined Hansford on a factory 602L and Hansford won both legs, with DuHamel third and second for second overall. Although he only contested three rounds Hansford ended seventh in the FIM 750 Championship.

BARRY DITCHBURN

At the start of 1974, Barry Ditchburn was working part time in his father's steel fabrications factory and racing Yamahas part time for Ted Broad, but a dramatic turn around a year later saw him as a full-time rider for the Boyer Kawasaki Team. Although he began in the shadow of Mick Grant, Ditchburn soon proved he was no mere back-up rider. His 12-second win over Barry Sheene at Mallory Park in 1975 before 20,000 fans was rated by Sheene as the only time he was outridden. As Sheene says, 'Ditchburn beat me fair and square and there were no real excuses on my part.' Although Peter Agg at Suzuki offered Ditchburn a ride for 1976 he decided to stay with Kawasaki, but only after they matched the Suzuki offer.

Born in Northfleet, Kent in January 1949, Barry Ditchburn was the son of 1940s grass track racer Harry Ditchburn and nephew of ex-Spurs and England goalkeeper Ted Ditchburn. Barry began racing a Triton at his local circuit of Brands Hatch during the mid-1960s and from this he graduated to the Ted Broad Yamaha and riding to second in the 1973 British 750 Championship. Ditchburn's big break came after he won the 1974 Thruxton 400-mile race and landed a contract with Stan Shenton for 1975. While this was initially criticised, Shenton's faith in the modest Ditchburn was vindicated during 1975. His results during 1976 though were marred by crashes and retirements, apart from the last big race of the season, the Powerbike International at Brands Hatch, where he beat Phil Read, Grant and Sheene. Ditchburn remained with Kawasaki for 1977 but this was one of his more disappointing seasons and he wasn't re-signed for 1978. However, for 1979 he was again provided with factory support, but this time only machines (a KR250, KR350 and a KR750) were provided and he had to pay all expenses. That saw the end of a distinguished career with Kawasaki that always promised more than it delivered. As Ditchburn himself notes, 'I was always happy to stay out of the limelight and in those days we just didn't know enough about suspension and chassis set-up. If it wasn't right we just rode around the problem.' In 1981, Ditchburn emigrated to Australia where he engaged in sidecar racing, winning the 1989 Australian title.

Right: Barry Ditchburn and Stan Shenton examine the newly delivered 602L early in 1977. The rear shock absorbers were more layed down on this model.
(Barry Ditchburn)

Opposite: Although he didn't win, one of Hansford's finest rides was at the F750 race at Brands Hatch in 1978 where he almost overtook the entire field after crashing.
(Mick Woollett)

1978

For the 1978 Daytona 200, the AMA imposed an intake-area restriction to limit the performance of the 750cc racers and with three 27mm restrictor plates now required the KR750 was severely disadvantaged over the Yamahas with their 23mm restrictors. Not only did this see a considerable power reduction, but there wasn't enough power to match the traction of the new Goodyear 1705 tyre. Thus only a late decision saw Hansford and Doyle front up and Hansford was the only non-Yamaha qualifier. Again though, strong riding saw Hansford finish fifth.

Hansford remained as Kawasaki's sole hope in the FIM 750 World Championship and without the AMA restrictors continued to surprise the Yamaha-mounted field. At the second round at Imola a sixth and fourth in the two legs gave him fourth overall, Neville Doyle managing to get the 602L running faster than most could have imagined. 'By 1978 the KR750 was a three-year old bike that was out-of-date to begin with but I managed to get the power differential down to only about five horsepower less than the Yamaha,' Neville Doyle told the author.

Hansford led from the start at Paul Ricard but crashed on the 41st lap when his Michelin tyres lost traction. Still, even with this DNF, Hansford had enough points for fourth place in the three-round AGV Helmets World Cup. The 750 World Championship continued at Brands Hatch where Hansford rode one of the most spectacular races of his career. After an entanglement with Steve Baker for the lead at Druids Hansford outbraked almost the entire field to finish fourth in the first heat. As Neville Doyle recounts, 'the tight British circuits were similar to those in Australia and the emphasis on hard braking suited his style. By this stage we were using Brembo brakes.' In the second heat Hansford was leading Kenny Roberts when he struck a back marker, but he had the consolation of setting the fastest lap.

At the Österreichring in Austria Hansford survived a spectacular 125mph slide on the last lap, only to crash trying to overcome the speed disadvantage. He came fifth in the second heat. A wet Hockenheim gave Hansford some respite against the speed of the Yamahas and he finished second in the first heat, also setting the fastest

One of the great rider/tuner combinations in the history of Kawasaki road racing: Neville Doyle tends to Hansford's KR750 at Assen in 1978. Hansford won the first F750 race. *(Australian Motorcycle News)*

GREGG HANSFORD

Epitomising the blonde and bleached Australian, Brisbane-born Greggory John Hansford made his Kawasaki road racing debut on a 100cc motocross bike in 1971. He was only 17 and a few weeks later obtained his road riding licence. He worked as a motorcycle mechanic after leaving school, operating a motorcycle sales and repair business before becoming a professional motorcycle racer. After progressing to an H1-R and H2 in 1972 Hansford's improvement was meteoric and he won his first state title later in 1972. On a Yamaha for 1973 he then went on to win the Australian Unlimited Championship ahead of Ron Toombs on the new H2-R. Repeating this in 1974 Neville

Doyle then hired Hansford to ride for Team Kawasaki Australia for 1975.

After winning nearly everything in Australia, Hansford won 57 races from 64 starts in 1977, he rejected an offer to race cars. He had already driven a Ford touring car on occasion during 1977 but chose instead to go to Europe. 'To seriously improve we needed to go to contest the World Championships,' says Neville Doyle, 'but it was a huge step for Hansford and he initially had some trouble adjusting to it.' While ideally suited to the 750, Hansford's size always hindered him on the smaller KR250 and KR350. According to Neville Doyle, 'he was unbeatable if everything was right. The slightest problem would see him drop back and eventually retire. He only rode to win but winning world championships is about consistency. Unfortunately, Gregg just wasn't interested in racing for fourth or sixth.' Courted by Suzuki for 1979, and Yamaha for 1980, Hansford remained loyal to Neville Doyle and Kawasaki. As an active participant in the breakaway World Series movement Hansford's career was also disturbed during 1980.

In 1980, he married Julie, a former surf beauty queen, but his motorcycle racing came to an end during the Belgian Grand Prix at Spa in July 1981. After changing a front wheel on his KR500 during the race as rain began to fall, Hansford took to the track again only to find the front brakes inoperable as he came to the first tight corner. Taking the escape road he ran into a marshal's car, breaking his femur in the same leg that he broke at Imola only months earlier. Only 29 years of age, blood clots in his thigh saw Hansford out of action for five years. With ten GP wins he was one of the most talented racers not to win a world championship. Later, he became a touring car driver, winning the 1993 Bathurst 1000. After seven years as a part-time driver, he had only just gained a fulltime professional drive when he died in a freak accident in a Ford Mondeo at Phillip Island in Australia on 5 March 1995. He was only 42 years old.

lap. Drier conditions for race two saw him fourth but he still ended third overall. Date clashes with the Grands Prix meant Hansford missed the next round but he was back in contention at Assen where he comfortably won the first heat. He also looked like winning the second race when his front tyre slid away. With Hansford deciding to concentrate on the 250 and 350 World Championship he forewent the final two F750 events, but DuHamel represented Kawasaki at Mosport. DuHamel showed that he was still a highly competitive rider with a third and fifth for a third overall.

In the annual Transatlantic race series only Mick

Grant was KR750-mounted, and while he finished every race his best result was a fourth place. Grant again contested the British Superbike Championship, and now British Kawasaki's only representative. Sidemm-backed Frenchman Bernard Fau joined him at every round and while they achieved reasonable results there were no victories that year. Grant ended third in the Championship. Grant though was again devastating at the Isle of Man, again winning the 1,000cc Classic TT, this time at an average speed of 112.406mph (180.9km/h) with a new outright lap record of 114.333mph (184.001km/h).

1979

By 1979, the KR750 was struggling against a field of Yamahas but, with the new four-cylinder 602S on the horizon, Kawasaki gave factory support for Mike Baldwin in the USA and Gregg Hansford in Europe. In the UK, after a year on a Sid Griffiths Yamaha, Barry Ditchburn was also provided with two KR750s. However, that was the limit of his assistance and he still had to pay all costs and preparation. It was obvious that by now Kawasaki's interest in persevering with the KR750 was half-hearted.

As the only official US Kawasaki rider, Baldwin went to Daytona with a team led by Dennis David. Randy Hall was chief mechanic, assisted by Jeff Shetler and Martin Carney. A crash in practice and a broken collarbone saw him start from the back of the grid, but he astounded everyone by finishing fourth in the 200-miler. His KR750 was basically unchanged from 1978, but developments included slant-plug cylinder heads with extra intake length to accommodate the long restrictors. With a rev limit of 9,500rpm to save the crank, power was about 9 per cent below the best figure achieved before restrictors, but there was no denying that the restrictors hurt the three-cylinder machines more than the fours. Unfortunately, a crash at Laconia in June left Baldwin with a badly broken leg and this was the end of his career on the KR750.

Although concentrating on the 250 and 350cc World Championships Hansford found the time to race in some non-conflicting Formula 750 events early in the season. Again he surprised many but as Neville Doyle commented, 'the design was out-of-date when we got it and it was a headache to make it competitive.' While outpaced on the faster circuits Hansford was still a force on the tighter short circuits and came second overall at Brands Hatch. He then won the second leg at Nogaro in France, while Christian Estrosi came second overall on another KR750, with a second and third place.

At Easter, Graeme Crosby finished second in the Unlimited Australian Grand Prix at Bathurst and subsequently took his borrowed TKA KR750 to England where he raced it occasionally in rounds of the British Superbike Championship. In this championship Barry

Ditchburn struggled all season, his best result being a third at his home track, Brands Hatch. Ditchburn was also the last to race a KR750, at an international meeting at Brands Hatch on 23 October. There he finished third, but a month earlier Hansford gave the KR750 its final international victory. Representing the Rest of the World on KR750s in the AGV Nations Cup Hansford and Graeme Crosby finished first and second against Italy at Donington, their consistency giving the team overall victory. This final win was a fitting end to the KR750's racing career. The design may have been obsolete from the outset, but the KR750 provided Kawasaki with some of their most important racing results, and did much to promote the company's performance image.

New Zealand rider Graeme Crosby was one of the last to achieve success on the KR750 and is seen at Bathurst 1979 where he came second in the Australian Unlimited TT.
(Australian Motorcycle News)

THE 602S 'TRAPEZOID' FOUR

As soon as the development of the KR250 tandem twin was completed in early 1977 work progressed on designing a replacement 750. Code-named the 602S, this was to be a four-cylinder liquid-cooled two-stroke. Kawasaki engineers analysed the Yamaha TZ750 and concluded that they needed a narrower engine unit, and one that provided more freedom regarding transfer port size and placement, and exhaust. The result was a 'Trapezoid' four-cylinder engine layout consisting of four individual cylinders with the outside cylinders shifted forward. Two prototype engines were built during 1978, but the project was almost abandoned in October when the FIM announced that 1979 would be the final year that Formula 750 would have World Championship status.

Unlike the KR250, Kawasaki engineers eschewed rotary valve induction in favour of reed valves. They reasoned that the power benefits achieved by rotary valves were unnecessary in Formula 750, and the increase in motor width from side-mounted carburettors was detrimental. With considerable experience already gained from reed valves in motocross it was the KX125A4 that formed the basis of the 602S. The independent water-jacketed cylinders minimised internal hot spots and allowed virtually unlimited freedom of transfer port size and placement. The exhaust port was fully open and the staggered cylinders provided room underneath for the expansion chambers. The widest dimension across the engine was the front cylinders, 50mm narrower than the KR750, with the engine cases 20mm narrower. Each of the four crankshafts was supported at the outer end by a ball bearing and at the inner end by a caged roller bearing. The con-rods, with caged needle rollers, were similar to the KX125. Connecting the two outer cylinders was a cross-shaft with a central spur gear, this meshing with the drive gears on the inside ends of the rear cylinder crankshafts. A primary jackshaft took the drive to the dry clutch, similar to that

The design of the 602S engine placed the countershaft sprocket very close to the swingarm pivot, and the cylinder layout allowed the centre exhaust pipes to be tucked up underneath and clear of the outer pipes.
(Greg McBean/Two Wheels)

Neville Doyle had Campagnolo produce a special 4.60x18-inch cast magnesium wheel so as to mount the widest tyre then available, a Michelin 16/70. (Greg McBean/Two Wheels)

of the KR750 but larger in diameter, with stronger springs, and a rack and pinion release mechanism to reduce transmission width. The water pump was driven by a spur gear inside the No. 4 crankshaft and ignition was by a modified KR250 unit sitting on the outside of the No. 2 crank. An important feature was accessibility and the gearbox case could be removed separately. Also contributing to accessibility was the design of the frame that incorporated the engine as a stressed member. The estimated power was in the region of 143bhp at 10,500rpm, certainly enough to be competitive if both the class and development had proceeded.

When it came to designing a chassis for the new engine Kawasaki turned to Neville Doyle in Australia. Doyle secured the services of Kawasaki UK mechanic Jim Fitzgerald and work commenced in January 1979. Apart from using the engine as a fully stressed member, the frame was similar to that of the KR750, but with wider front frame downtubes and a shorter swingarm.

The countershaft sprocket was 30mm closer to the swingarm pivot and the fork rake increased half a degree to 28°. The trail was 100mm (up from 97mm) and the wheelbase was increased marginally. The weight too was up by around 5kg. Although the suspension was from the KR750 Doyle commissioned Campagnolo to build a special, 4.60x18-inch magnesium wheel to take a wider Michelin tyre. At that stage this was the widest wheel fitted to a conventional motorcycle. The front, 18-inch, wheel also pioneered the incorporation of the brake disc carriers.

Three weeks before its projected race debut at Mugello, Hansford tried the completed machine at Calder Park in Australia. This test was encouraging enough, but at practice at Mugello excessive vibration saw Hansford revert to the older triple. The machine then went back to Japan and no more was heard of it. Coming at the end of the life of Formula 750 racing, the 602S promised much, but appeared too late.

4 AIR-COOLED FOURS IN ENDURANCE AND SUPERBIKE

Eddie Lawson's 1981 AMA Championship-winning KZ1000 Superbike. Although ostensibly based on a production KZ1000J there was a large number of exotic components. The front brakes were from the KR500 Grand Prix. *(Cycle World)*

Although Kawasaki had shown some interest in Endurance racing back in 1969, when 500cc H1s took out second and third in the Bol d'Or, it wasn't until the release of the Z1 in 1972 that they had a suitable machine as a basis for Endurance racing. Long distance Endurance racing was particularly popular in Europe, and with an expansion of interest in the European market, from 1974 Kawasaki began to place more emphasis on this racing genre.

The high specification of the Z1 engine made it ideal for Endurance racing. The engine was also in a very mild state of tune and plainly over engineered, as demonstrated at Daytona on 14 March 1973 when 45 speed and Endurance records were set by three specially prepared Z1s ridden by a team that included Yvon DuHamel, Gary Nixon, and Hurley Wilvert.

It wasn't long before Endurance racing specialists in Europe adopted the Z1 as an alternative to the Honda 750 four and early in 1973 Christian Leon and Jean-François Baldé won the Le Mans 1,000-kilometre race on a specially prepared Z1. At the most prestigious event, the Bol d'Or, the French Kawasaki importer Sidemm supplied selected teams with special machines. These Yoshimura-tuned engines produced 96bhp and featured 31mm carburettors, Yoshimura camshafts, and close ratio gearboxes. Sidemm brought out Yoshimura junior and works mechanics, and Renouf and René Guili came second. Z1s also came fourth and fifth, this encouraging result leading to more direct factory support for 1974.

1974

For 1974, former Honda Endurance riders Georges Godier and Alain Genoud teamed with Swiss frame builder Fritz Egli to build a Z1-based Endurance racer. With a 69mm Yoshimura kit giving 987cc and racing camshafts, valves and gearbox, the engine was mounted in an Egli chassis. This featured a large (4in) single backbone tube and was extremely compact. The steering head was only 737mm (29in) from the ground and the wheelbase 1,397mm (55in). There were Marzocchi forks, twin Koni rear shock absorbers, and Lockheed brakes. While making only around 80bhp at the rear wheel, the engine produced a lot of torque, and with a moderate weight of only 180kg the Godier/Genoud Egli Kawasaki provided the best combination of power, handling, and reliability.

At the Barcelona 24-hour race at the twisting Montjuich Park, Godier and Genoud won at an average speed of 73.15mph (118km/h), following this with a win in the 1,000km race at Mettet and a second in the Spa 24-hour race. At the most important event on the Endurance calendar, the Bol d'Or, Godier and Genoud won at an average speed of 74.93mph (121km/h). Eighteen Kawasakis made the grid, including the official Yoshimura machines from Sidemm. These were provided to Yvon DuHamel and Christian Leon, as well as Percy Tait and Jean-François Baldé, and featured linked front and rear discs. Nine of the 23 finishers were Kawasakis and Guili and Gerard Choukroun came second, with William Gougy and Gilles Husson fourth.

Jacques Luc rode a specially prepared Yoshimura Z1 Endurance racer at the 1973 Bol d'Or at Le Mans.
(Mick Woollett)

1975

Godier and Genoud had a radically new machine for the 1975 Endurance series, with the 1,000cc Z1-based engine now housed in a special triangulated tubular steel frame that wrapped around the engine. Four tubes supported the 75mm steering head and connected it to a conventional engine cradle and lateral tubes to aluminium alloy plates behind the gearbox. The frame structure was constructed of ultra thin-wall steel (25 CD 4S) and incorporated a triangulated swingarm that weighed only 2.26kg and operated a single Koni Formula 1 car shock absorber through a bell-crank. Unlike other designs at that time the vertical shock absorber was mounted under the gearbox and provided a 5.25:1 rising rate to give 76mm of wheel travel for a suspension movement of only 14mm. At the front were 38mm Ceriani forks with 290mm Brembo front disc brakes.

The entire machine was designed with easy access and Endurance racing in mind. Holding 31 litres of fuel and fitted with gravity and quick fillers, the tank unit was quickly detachable. Two bolts located the moulded seat unit that looked to be composite with the tank. The three-piece fairing could be removed in only 12 seconds and all the electrics, including the fuel pump, were housed in a unit in front of the fuel tank. Apart from revisions to the cylinder head there were few developments to the 1,000cc engine which was in a modest state of tune. With Keihin 31mm carburettors and a Devil four-into-one exhaust system it provided a reliable 100bhp at the crankshaft. The new Endurance racer weighed more than its Egli predecessor at 200kg, and while the team had a slow start to the season, again won the Bol d'Or. This was Kawasaki's best result ever in this prestigious race, Godier and Genoud leading the Cassegrain Kawasaki of Christian Estrosi and Husson, with DuHamel and Baldé third on a Sidemm-Godier-Genoud machine. Godier and Genoud also set a new race record of 77.375mph (124.5km/h) covering 1,857 miles (2,988.56km). Jacques Luc and Alain Vial then gave Kawasaki their second Endurance victory for 1975 by winning the Thruxton 400 Miles. Godier and Genoud finished third, narrowly giving them their fourth *Coupe d'Endurance*.

Alain Genoud working on the 1974 Egli-Kawasaki Endurance racer.
(Two Wheels)

GODIER AND GENOUD

A Frenchman living in Switzerland during the early 1970s, Georges Godier was born in 1935 and was a motorcycle mechanic by trade. He had raced a Norton 750 in hill-climbs before meeting Alain Genoud, a Swiss barman equally interested in motorcycles. The two then teamed together and in 1972 won the FIM *Coupe d'Endurance* on their Honda Japuto 1000. They repeated this in 1973, and went into the 1974 season as the most experienced Endurance team. Along with Fritz Egli they created an Endurance racer good enough to give Kawasaki their first European *Coupe d'Endurance*, despite a limited budget.

The 1975 Godier/Genoud Endurance racer came about after two engineers, Pierre Doncque from Amiens University, and Michel Lambert a practising engineer, approached Xavier Maugendra of Sidemm for financial support to develop a completely new chassis for the Z1. Initially sceptical, it was only when Godier showed enthusiasm for the concept that Maugendra decided to support it. Work progressed throughout the winter of

1974/75 and the essence of the design was that the entire machine be an integral unit specifically built for Endurance racing. For the design of the frame Doncque was able to use the computer at Amiens University, as well input from his students when it came to calculations. Although they enjoyed support from Sidemm through until 1977, for 1978 this wasn't forthcoming and Godier then prepared several machines for the Kool-sponsored team. Godier and Genoud maintained their association with Kawasaki France through the 1980s, and were instrumental in winning the World Championship in 1982. When Kawasaki withdrew from racing Godier and Genoud kept the flag flying in the French Streetbike series with an overbored GPz900R. They were later involved in the return to Endurance racing and the preparation of the World Superbike GPX750R. Not only quick on the track, Georges Godier always had a reputation as a fast road rider and was killed in a road accident in April 1993 while riding a Turbo Kawasaki.

1976–79

Right: The Z1 dominated the Australian Castrol Six-hour race for production motorcycles for many years. Kenny Blake rides to victory in 1973. (*Australian Motorcycle News*)

Opposite: Yvon DuHamel and Jean-François Baldé led much of the 1976 Bol d'Or on the Godier-Genoud Z1 Endurance racer.
(*Two Wheels*)

THE CASTROL SIX-HOUR PRODUCTION RACE

One of the more unusual events during the 1970s was the Australian Castrol Six-hour race for stock production motorcycles. Held at Amaroo Park near Sydney, this event was televised live across the nation and the organisers, the Willoughby District Motor Cycle Club, strictly enforced production regulations. Kawasakis figured prominently, and in 1972, the first year with Castrol sponsorship, Mike Steele and Dave Burgess won on an H2. The following year the superior fuel consumption of the Z1 saw victory in the hands of Kenny Blake who raced the full six hours solo. Always dogged by controversy, the 1974 race saw Len Atlee and Kenny Blake judged the winners on their Z1 after three of the first four place getters were disqualified. The same year there was also a similar event in New Zealand, held at the Manfeild circuit, Ginger Molloy riding a Z1 to victory.

Another dramatic race in 1975 saw Hansford and Sayle triumphant on their Z1 following the retirement of John Warrian's Ducati 900 Super Sport just before the end of the race. Over in New Zealand too the Z1 remained unbeatable in the hands of Graeme Crosby. There was less contention in 1976 when Roger Heyes and Jim Budd virtually led from start to finish on their Z1B, while in New Zealand, Graeme Crosby took the new Z1000 to an easy victory. He repeated this in 1977, sharing the Z1000 with Tony Hatton. Results were lean for the Z1000 over the next few years, although in 1978, Rob Phillis teamed with Rick Perry to win the 750cc class on a Z650C. Future 500cc World Champion Wayne Gardner repeated this with John Pace in the 1979 event.

After a tentative effort during 1975, Honda came into Endurance racing with full factory RCB racers for 1976, and there was little Kawasaki could do to stop the onslaught without equal factory support. Even though their chassis was still at the forefront of motorcycle design, by 1976 the Godier/Genoud Z1 had reached the limit of engine development so the team resorted to weight saving and carburettor experimentation. Keihin racing carburettors were installed but Godier couldn't use CV carburettors like the Honda because they weren't available in the size that he required. Gravity fuel feed replaced the electric pump, and to overcome ground clearance problems the machine was raised 35mm at the rear and 40mm at the front through longer front forks. Because the engine was now difficult to start, an alternator and started motor were fitted. At high speed circuits such as Spa, wilder camshafts were tried, but with the standard valve springs these failed, and softer Yoshimura camshafts were used at the Bol d'Or, with the valve seats lowered to reduce the risk of the valves touching the pistons. The weight was reduced to 167kg, and with Yoshimura camshafts and electronic ignition from a 700 Yamaha, the power was 102bhp at 9,000rpm at the rear wheel. Godier estimated the power to be 110–115bhp at the crankshaft, still somewhat down on that of the Honda.

At the non-championship Le Mans 1,000km race, Baldé and Husson won on a fuel-injected semi-works Z1, but in the *Coupe d'Endurance* the Godier-Genoud Kawasakis were outclassed. With Godier and Genoud now team managers, Luc and Vial finished third at Mugello and sixth at Montjuich. At Bol d'Or, the Sidemm-sponsored Kawasakis almost defeated the Hondas. DuHamel again teamed with Baldé and looked set for victory 18 hours into the race. Then the Honda of Chemarin and Alex George overtook them and they eventually finished third. Christian Sarron and Denis Boulom came second, with Luc and Vial sixth, enough to give them third in the final standings.

For 1977, Kawasaki still had no answer to the Honda RCB and without factory support the Kawasaki effort lacked real strength. Godier and

Top: With its upright riding position and high handlebars Graeme Crosby's Moriwaki Z1 took the 1979 British Formula 1 Championship by storm. (*Australian Motorcycle News*)

Bottom: By 1978, the only Kawasaki that could stay with the RCB Hondas was the Pipart machine of John-Bernard Peyre and Maurice Maingret. Maingret lines up at Liège where they finished second. (*Australian Motorcycle News*)

Genoud resumed their position as riders, retiring at Misano. Most effort was concentrated on the Bol d'Or, with Baldé and Michel Frutschi joining Godier and Genoud. Again, Godier and Genoud were performing strongly but it was Baldé and Frutschi who gave Kawasaki their best result of the season with a second place. Although the Z1 was no longer an outright winner in Endurance racing, it was still a popular choice amongst privateers during 1978. The Pipart Kawasaki of John-Bernard Peyre and Maurice Maingret was the only Kawasaki that could stay with the Hondas and they finished second at Liège and fourth in the Bol d'Or. The Pipart Kawasaki used a cantilever rear suspension with a single de Carbon damper but the engine was now too wide, limiting ground clearance and increasing frontal area. Also achieving good results during 1978 was the National Moto Kawasaki. In the hands of Roger Ruiz and Richard Hubin this finished the season second in the manufacturers' title. John Cowie and Bernie Toleman were also amongst the leading privateers on their Peckett and McNab Kawasaki, taking the British Formula 1 Championship.

After dominating Endurance racing for three years, Honda significantly reduced their effort for 1979, allowing the Performance Kawasaki of Christian Huguet and Hervé Moineau to reassert itself. Their Z1000-based engine bristled with factory parts, including a special crankshaft, and they won the six-hour race at Assen. A second place at Barcelona and another victory at Brands Hatch saw Huguet finish third overall with Kawasaki second in the manufacturers' championship. For the prestigious, but non-championship, Bol d'Or at Paul Ricard, Kork Ballington teamed with Baldé to finish seventh.

One of the most spectacular racing Kawasakis of 1979 was New Zealander Graeme Crosby's 994cc Moriwaki Formula 1 machine. Campaigned in the British Formula 1 Championship Crosby surprised many with his sit-up-and-beg riding style. Crosby finished second in the championship, and fourth in the Isle of Man Formula 1 TT.

AMA SUPERBIKE PRODUCTION 1975–80

Although Yvon DuHamel won the first 'Superbike' race in the USA, an exhibition event at Laguna Seca in 1973 on a Yoshimura Z1, it wasn't until 1975 that production racing became popular in that country. The same year, Dave Aldana won the Heavyweight Production race at Daytona, with Z1s filling the first three places. Later in the season, DuHamel won the Heavyweight Production class at Laguna Seca and Ontario on a Dale-Starr-prepared Z1. Here was a class that was ideally suited to the Z1, and one that would develop to become the premier racing class in the USA. In 1976, the regulations changed and the class became Superbike Production, with more modification allowed. This year the Z1s were too 'stock' to compete with the highly modified European twins. Horsepower wasn't a problem with those early Z1 Superbikes, but taming the street chassis with slick tyres was always a challenge. It wasn't until reigning Superbike Champion Reg Pridmore switched to a Pierre DesRoches Racecrafters Kawasaki that the Z1 took out its first AMA Superbike victory, at Pocono in 1977. Pridmore went on to win the 1977 AMA Superbike Production crown.

For 1978, rule changes favoured the four-cylinder machines as alternators, headlights, standard bodywork and muffler shells were no longer necessary. With Vetter sponsorship Pridmore stayed with DesRoches who remanufactured the production frame to obtain the necessary rigidity for racing. He also had Rob North install a larger diameter steering head to accommodate Yamaha TZ750 tapered roller bearings. Engine development included 70mm cast 11.8:1 Yoshimura pistons, 37.5mm Manley stainless steel inlet valves, Yoshimura Bonneville camshafts, a C. R. Axtell flowed cylinder head and bored (to 31mm), and heavily modified standard Mikuni carburettors. Adapting a Bassani Superbike exhaust system saw the measured rear wheel horsepower at 141.5bhp at 9,000rpm. The wheels were Morris magnesium, a WM4x19-inch on the front and a WM7x19-inch on the rear, shod with Dunlop slick

tyres. From the KR750 came the front brake calipers and master cylinder. Although still having too much power for the chassis and not managing to win a single National during the season, Pridmore's consistency again gave him the AMA Superbike Production Championship.

Superbike racing took a big step in 1979 when Kawasaki hired the young professional rider Mike Baldwin. Previously, Superbike was a class for serious and enthusiastic amateurs and Kawasaki, as the first Japanese manufacturer to become directly involved in Superbike racing, provided Baldwin with a pair of Yoshimura-engined KZ1000 Mk IIs. One of these started life as a 1975 KZ900 and was purchased from Yoshimura R&D for only $5,000. The KZ1000 Mk IIs featured Lockheed, and later, KR750 brakes, Morris wheels and Goodyear tyres. Injuries sidelined Baldwin after Loudon and his machine was then ridden by rising star Freddie Spencer. Although Spencer ran away with the races at Sears Point and Laguna Seca the cancellation of the final two events separated Spencer from the Superbike title. The era of the professional Superbike rider had begun and this would see a quantum leap forward in the quality of the

Reg Pridmore won his third AMA Superbike Championship, and his second on a Kawasaki, on the DesRoches Vetter Z1.

(Two Wheels)

machinery over the next few years.

With the factory Suzuki and Hondas lining up alongside the Kawasakis in 1980 the Z1000 racers were placed under even more pressure. The Daytona Superbike race was extended to 100 miles and newly signed factory Kawasaki rider Eddie Lawson had a KHI-supplied KZ1000, while Hansford raced the 1979 California-built model. Lawson's machine (tuned by Randy Hall) had twin spark plug cylinder heads to reduce detonation and, with the power around 140bhp, they had special swingarms able to accommodate the new Goodyear 3.85x18 tyres. The entire rear wheel assembly was from a KR750. This machine was also entered in the AFM Ontario Six-hour race, where Lawson and Aldana finished officially second, although this was disputed as Kawasaki believed they had won. At the Talladega Superbike race Lawson and Aldana finished first and second. Lawson won again at Road Atlanta and Pocono and went to the final race at Daytona needing to finish seventh to win his first AMA Superbike Championship (and a $30,000 contingency bonus). The disqualification of Wes Cooley saw Lawson initially awarded the championship, but this was overruled two months later.

Opposite: Jim Budd testing the Z1000SR at Oran Park in early 1980, prior to Endurance racing in Australia. *(Two Wheels)*

Right: Mike Baldwin's Z1000 Mk II at Daytona in 1979. This was the first official factory Superbike. *(Two Wheels)*

1980

New Endurance regulations saw the adoption of more restrictive production-based TT Formula 1 rules, and with the Endurance series being granted World Championship status there was renewed interest by Kawasaki. Although there was still freedom allowed with chassis design, 1,000cc four-strokes with a standard stroke, crankcase, cylinder, cylinder head castings, and carburettors were required. The French withdrew their events (including the Bol d'Or) from the championship in protest at the new regulations, but it was still the French Performance team of Christian Huguet and Richard Hubin that spearheaded Kawasaki's effort.

As a prelude to the Endurance series, a factory Z1000SR was sent to Australia in March to contest two Endurance events, the Coca Cola 800 at Oran Park and the Arai 500 at Bathurst. This 998cc prototype produced around 140bhp, and featured a KR750-based frame (with larger diameter thinner walled tubes), and a KR500-style braced aluminium swingarm. The weight was 168kg. Hansford teamed with Jim Budd for the Coca Cola 800 race but retired with ignition failure while leading comfortably. The Endurance Performance Kawasaki was similar in specification to the prototype Z1000SR and finished second at the Sterreichring 1,000km race. It was at the Suzuka Eight-hour race, the first World Championship event in Japan since the mid-Sixties, that Kawasaki put in the most effort, Gregg Hansford teaming with Eddie Lawson. Their Z1000SR now featured a single rear shock absorber, but according to Neville Doyle, this was very difficult to set up. Hansford and Lawson finished second, although Lawson was leading until he ran over Mike Cole who crashed in front of him. Lawson sportingly stopped to make sure that Cole was unharmed and lost the lead to Crosby. The developments on the Suzuka machine found their way on to the Performance Kawasaki of Huguet and Hubin and they won the final Endurance round at Misano. With the Bol d'Or at Paul Ricard, a non-championship event that year, the factory provided prototype machines for Hansford and Budd and the Performance team. The engine was increased to 1,134cc (74x66mm) but there were problems with holing pistons. After lowering the compression on Huguet and Hubin's machine they finished third, and were placed third overall in the Endurance World Championship.

DRAG RACING

Motorcycle drag racing, primarily an American racing culture, was the preserve of Harley-Davidson until the early 1970s. By 1973 other makes had begun to make inroads, including Kawasaki, and during 1975 Denco Performance constructed a triple-engined H2 drag racer for Boris Murray. With each engine displacing 792cc and fed by a bank of Denco-Mikuni 38mm carburettors, the 360bhp Denco H2 ran in the Top Fuel class at Fremont, winning first time out with a quarter mile in 8.60 seconds and 169.84mph (273.27km/h). In the Pro-Stock category Bob Carpenter began a long association with Kawasaki, winning the Number One plate in 1974 aboard an H2. Carpenter switched to a Z1 for 1975, setting a Pro-Stock class record of 9.50 seconds at 138.88mph (223.46km/h). That year, Terry Vance won the Number One plate, also on a Z1.

In Europe, the Z1 also began to assert itself in drag racing through the efforts of the Dutch importer Henk Vink. Vink supercharged a 975cc Z1 'Big Spender 4' and set a standing start quarter mile time of 9.00 seconds at 160mph (257km/h) during 1975. Vink later built a twin-engined dragster and had the fastest drag motorcycle in Europe until 1981. He then returned to a single supercharged 1,356cc engine that produced around 300bhp and managed to get his 500lb machine to cover the quarter mile in eight seconds with a terminal speed of 180mph (290km/h).

In the USA, Z1-based machines continued to set records and during 1978 Mike Bruso, on a Denco 1,198cc Z1000 stock dragbike, went 8.89 seconds at 152mph (245km/h). Also that year Don Vesco also gave Kawasaki the title of the 'World's Fastest Motorcycle' with a speed of 318.598mph (512.62km/h) on a twin-KZ1000-engined turbocharged streamliner. Carpenter again earned the Pro-Stock Number One plate in 1979, along with Kawasaki's $10,000 contingency bonus, while Sid Pogue won the IDBA Pro-Stock Championship. The IDBA (International Drag Bike Association) was a separate faction to the NMRA (National Motorcycle Racing Association) which became absorbed by the NHRA (National Hot Rod Association) when motorcycles were included in car events after 1978.

During 1980, Bo O'Brochta took out the Top Fueler and Mike Bruso the Super Eliminator categories on Z1000-based machines. O'Brochta was the quickest in the world with a time of 7.08 seconds at 197mph (316.97km/h). His 1,200cc supercharged Z1 (23lb boost) produced around 400hp on 89 per cent nitro-methane fuel, and featured a two-speed transmission with a compressed-air gear change. O'Brochta continued to dominate Top Fuel racing through 1981. During 1982, 'Superbike Mike' Keyte set a Pro-Stock class record of 8.71 seconds at 154.63mph (248.8km/h). Then followed a period where Suzuki engines were favoured over the Kawasaki in Pro-Stock.

In September 1983, Elmer Trett broke the 200mph barrier with his Top-Fuel Z1000-based machine with a 7.16 second, 201.34mph (324km/h) quarter mile run. A crash in 1984 contributed to the banishment by the NHRA of Top Fuel nitro methane-burning machines to exhibition-only status. During 1989, Trett put his 'Mountain Magic' Top Fueler through the quarter mile in 6.60 seconds at 213.77mph (343.96km/h), then the fastest time ever for a motorcycle. By 1990 he had improved this to 6.53 seconds at 219.09mph (352.52km/h). Trett's 1,327cc (80x66mm) supercharged Z1000 produced more than 800bhp. Few parts though were shared with the Z1000. The cylinder head was milled from solid billet, the one-piece crankshaft was by Moldex and the con-rods and main bearings from a small block Chevrolet. Known as the Father of Top Fuel, Trett was killed in an exhibition run at Indianapolis in 1996. Two weeks prior to his death he had set a quarter mile world record of 6.06 seconds at 235mph (378km/h), and died aiming to break into the five-second bracket.

In the 1992 Prostar Top Fuel/Funnybike Championship, Steve Rice won on a turbocharged, fuel-injected 1,260cc Z1. Using the stock crankshaft, cylinder head and engine cases of a then-current KZ1000P (police model), 45lb of turbo boost created 425bhp. Even by 1997, the KZ1000 was still a potent force with the Funnybike record of 6.74 seconds at 211mph (339km/h) being held by Gary Clark. It wasn't until Steve Rice began development of a ZX-11 Ninja-based drag bike during 1997 that the long-term dominance of the elderly bullet-proof KZ four was threatened.

1981

Kawasaki released the new Z1000J for 1981 and these improved engines formed the basis of the factory Endurance racers. Now with larger (magnesium-bodied) Mikuni 34mm carburettors, a revised combustion chamber and valve angle, as well as larger valves, these engines proved outstandingly reliable. KHI three-ring forged 69.99mm pistons provided a maximum allowable 1,015cc and the compression ratio was a moderate 10.2:1. The standard pressed up crankshaft was lightened by 25 per cent by removing material from the counterweights, and there were special tapers on the crankshaft to run the ignition on the left and alternator on the right. To reduce detonation, and overcome the difficulty of inferior racing fuel, twin spark plug ignition was employed.

The frame was similar to that of the previous year, and retained the single Kayaba shock absorber mounted on the right and at an acute angle. The front forks were also Kayaba and sometimes featured an anti-dive system similar to that of the KR500. On the front of the fork legs there was an external passageway and an additional reservoir to adjust the damping.

Serge Rosset's Performance team again represented Kawasaki in the Endurance World Championship, and partnering stalwarts Jean-Claude Chemarin and Christian Huguet were two young French racers, Raymond Roche and Jean Lafond. These two ex-GP riders finished every event, winning the Sterreichring 1,000km race and the Barcelona 24-hour race on their way to taking the World Championship. Their more experienced team-mates, Chemarin and Huguet, won the 24-hours at Le Mans and the Mugello 1,000km, giving Kawasaki their first Endurance title since 1975.

Superbike racing was different in the UK from the USA and was also open to racing two-strokes. In the *Motor Cycle News* Superbike Championship Wayne Gardner won at Cadwell Park on a Moriwaki Z1000, taking third in the Championship, but the big four-strokes were not really competitive with the Grand Prix machines. Roger Marshall also rode a Moriwaki Z1000, winning the Formula 1 race at Oliver's Mount and coming fourth in the TT F1 Championship, with Gardner fifth. Gardner went on to win the Australian Swann Series on the Moriwaki machine, his exploits earning him a Honda contract for 1982.

The 1981 Endurance racer featured a braced aluminium swingarm with a single Kayaba shock absorber. The Kayaba forks also included an external passageway and reservoir for adjustable damping. This machine gave Kawasaki their first Endurance World Championship since 1975. *(Author's collection)*

AMA SUPERBIKE PRODUCTION 1981–82

After two years struggling to match the Honda and Suzuki, Lawson's KZ1000J-based Superbike was finally up to the task for 1981. Rob Muzzy, a 39-year-old former drag bike and dirt-track engine builder from Oregon, was recruited as lead mechanic in January 1981 after answering an advertisement in *Cycle News*. By mid-season he was crew chief in charge of engine development. The 1,015cc engines came from KHI in Endurance racing trim and Muzzy substituted a Canadian model cylinder head without anti-pollution air breather passageways. The camshafts were from the Endurance machines and used KZ650-style shim retainers, while the titanium valves were slightly smaller at 38.5mm for the inlet and 32mm for the exhaust. Twin spark plug ignition was retained so that ignition advance could be reduced to 32°. The con-rods were stock, although Muzzy polished the leading edge to prevent breakage at high rpm. He also cut the taper off the left end of the lightened factory crankshaft and on the right installed the magneto flywheel and pickups from a KX80 motocrosser. The clutch was based on production parts but used a KZ1100 shaft-drive model centre hub and there was an improved gearshift mechanism and gearbox. With 36mm EI flat-slide carburettors (with Superbike-legal 31mm restrictors) and a Kerker exhaust system; by the end of the season the power was up to around 150bhp at 10,250rpm.

With the production chassis limiting development, the KZ1000J received an improved frame, with a set back, re-angled steering head, and backbone strengthening. Thus the Superbike frame was surprisingly stock but for a small gusset at the rear engine mount. The steering head angle was 27.5° and, as with the production bike, the engine was rubber-mounted in the front and rigidly mounted at the rear. The Kayaba air-assisted forks were fabricated in Santa Ana, California, with longer and thinner wall tubes and alternative triple clamps that provided different off-set. Regulations in 1981 allowed for changes behind the swingarm pivot so Randy Hall built a braced aluminium swingarm with KR500-style eccentric chain adjusters. This also came in different lengths to suit a particular circuit and the rear suspension was a pair of Works

Performance shock absorbers from a Maico motocrosser. The front discs were 313mm cast iron with magnesium carriers, with KR500 four-piston magnesium brake calipers. The rear 229mm disc was from the KR750, with a Lockheed caliper and the wheels were Morris magnesium, a WM4-18 on the front and WM8-18 on the rear. Superbikes in those days still weren't particularly light or short, and Lawson's KZ1000 weighed close to the minimum 188kg with a wheelbase of around 59in/1,500mm (depending on swingarm length). Muzzy's preparation and Lawson's riding disguised any deficiencies in the KZ1000 Superbike. Lawson didn't crash all year and after a slow start to the season won (with Ron Pierce) the AFM Six-hour race at Ontario. He went on to win Superbike races at Elkhart Lake, Loudon, Laguna Seca and Seattle to take the Championship by ten points from Honda-mounted Freddie Spencer. It was an amazing demonstration of confidence and consistency.

As the four-cylinder 1,000cc Superbikes were now even more powerful than the 750cc two-strokes, 1982 was the final year AMA Superbikes had a 1,025cc limit. Kawasaki's budget was a fraction of Honda's (a rumoured $300,000 compared with $3½ million) and at Daytona Eddie Lawson was clearly down on speed to the four-valve Hondas. He finished fifth, but by Talladega crew chief Muzzy and tuner Ken Funkhouser had found some more horsepower, and Lawson won. He won again at Riverside and Elkhart Lake, but new team-mate Wayne Rainey won at Loudon as Lawson slowed with handling and tyre troubles. Lawson won again at Laguna Seca, a day before crashing the KR500, breaking his seventh vertebrae. This sidelined him for two races, but amazingly, he came back to win at Seattle, astounding his doctors and the competition. All Lawson needed to do was to finish 14th at the final round at Palm Beach, and he took fifth using a stock KZ1000J engine. A leap in Honda horsepower at this stage of the season mattered little and Lawson won his second Superbike title. A development of the 1981 machine, the wheelbase of Lawson's bike was now 50mm shorter, and the emphasis was on broadening the powerband. Through careful attention to porting and

Opposite: Eddie Lawson demonstrating the style that made the combination of him, Muzzy and the KZ1000 Superbike unbeatable during 1981 and 1982. *(Cycle World)*

For 1982, Kawasaki Motors Corporation offered a small number of Eddie Lawson Replica KZ1000S Superbikes to privateers. They were very high specification machines, but because there was only one more season for 1,000cc Superbikes, they weren't as popular as anticipated. *(Cycle World)*

exhaust systems Muzzy still managed to extract 152bhp at 10,250rpm on their dyno. There were also new crankshafts with titanium con-rods and aluminium Electrofusion-coated cylinders. Crankshaft vibration was so extreme though that the crankcases and cylinders were bending, requiring solid copper cylinder base gaskets to overcome the leakage.

The front brakes were now larger diameter slotted discs with two-piston KR750 calipers, and the Superbike was also surprisingly effective in Formula 1. Lawson chose it in preference to the KR500 at New Hampshire and finished second. As Lawson said, 'those Superbikes were real predictable; you knew where the limit was. And the power was controllable and linear. But they were so big and heavy they just wore you out.' Considering the strong competition, Kawasaki's 1982 Superbike Championship further demonstrated Lawson's huge talent and the Muzzy's ability as a tuner. In the words of Eddie Lawson: 'If it wasn't for Rob we wouldn't have won those Superbike Championships; it wouldn't have happened.'

Following Eddie Lawson's 1981 Superbike victory, Kawasaki Motors Corporation offered 30 factory replica KZ1000S Superbikes to selected privateers. While most of the engine specifications were as with the Lawson bike, instead of the flat-slide EI carburettors, these 998cc (69.4x66mm) replicas had Keihin CR Special 33mm smoothbore carburettors. The 11.3:1 pistons were US-made and there were twin spark plugs per cylinder. The valve sizes were 38 and 32mm and the camshafts ground from pre-J hollowed exhaust billets. The lightened crankshaft repositioned the alternator on the right with the KX80 ignition. The chassis featured an aluminium swingarm with eccentric chain adjusters and the front braking by slotted front discs with KR750 twin-piston brake calipers. Only 17 KZ1000Ss were sold and they were the closest a privateer could get to a genuine factory bike. With 136bhp they were also very competitive. Wayne Rainey finished fourth at Daytona and Harry Klinzmann second at Sears Point on a KZ1000S. Klinzmann also teamed with Thad Wolff to win the Budweiser 500 race at Riverside.

The factory Z1000-based Endurance racers reached the peak of their development in 1982. Chemarin and Cornu won the Endurance World Championship, with Lafond and Guilleux second. This year there was Uni-Trak rear suspension and occasionally, a 16-inch front wheel.
(Mick Woollett)

1982

After winning the Endurance World Championship in 1981, it was no surprise to see Rosset's Performance Team again representing the factory. Still run under Formula 1 regulations, the engine width of the Z1000 engine was reduced by relocating the alternator behind the engine, now driven by a rubber belt. Chassis development included a Uni-Trak linkage rear suspension set-up, with the battery mounted underneath. The mechanical anti-dive, discarded on the KR500, was retained, and while an 18-inch front wheel was generally used there was also experimentation with a 16-inch.

In the team makeup Huguet retired, his position filled by the Swiss rider Jacques Cornu who now rode with Chemarin. With the departure of Roche to Honda, Hervé Guilleux joined Lafond on the second machine. At the opening round at Imola all the works machines boycotted the event due to inadequate lighting and too

many chicanes, but a Kawasaki still won. Gerry van Rooyan, the 'Flying Dutchwoman', and motorcycle racing's first transsexual, won with Marco Bonke on a Bakker Z1000.

Chemarin and Cornu showed at the Nürburgring Eight-hour race that they were still the team to beat and led almost the entire race. A factory boycott at Barcelona gave Kawasaki another victory, this time to Christian Berthod, Jean Monnin and Marc Granie, then at the Liège 24-hour race at Spa team orders saw Chemarin and Cornu cross the line first. Chemarin and Cornu went into the final race, the Bol d'Or with a small lead in the Championship. Here, in front of 200,000 spectators the Kawasakis did it in style, Lafond, Guilleux and Patrick Igoa winning, with Chemarin, Cornu and Sergio Pellandini second. Chemarin and Cornu won the Endurance World Championship, with Lafond and Guilleux second.

Top: Eddie Lawson and Rob Muzzy at the end of 1981, fresh from winning the AMA Superbike Championship. (Cycle World)

Bottom: Taking over from Eddie Lawson on the factory Superbike in the USA was the equally talented Wayne Rainey. On the seemingly obsolete GPz750 Rainey gave Kawasaki yet another AMA Superbike title. Rainey discusses the 750 with tuners Mark and Steve Johnson. (Cycle World)

EDDIE LAWSON

As a kid growing up in Ontario, Southern California, Eddie Lawson began riding a small Kawasaki dirt bike with his grandfather. Under the guidance of father Ray he was soon racing dirt track for Shell Thuett and Pete Pistoni. After a successful career in dirt track Lawson made the switch to road racing in 1977, promptly winning the Novice 250cc race at Daytona. A pivotal event of Lawson's career occurred towards the end of 1979 when Pierre des Roches let Eddie ride a Vetter Kawasaki Superbike in a club event. Lawson's ability astounded des Roches and Gary Mathers (KMC racing manager) who offered him a test on the factory Superbike. This led to the signing of the 20-year-old Lawson for the 1980 AMA Superbike Championship for $25,000. Although he only raced factory Kawasakis for three years Lawson was spectacularly successful, raising the company's racing profile in the USA and leading to the production of the KZ1000R Eddie Lawson Replica. Initially under the shadow of Freddie Spencer, Lawson earned the nickname 'Steady Eddie' but ultimately proved his star quality with four 500cc World Championships (1984, 1986, 1988 and 1989) and 31 500cc Grand Prix victories. He was also one of the few to win a World Championship in successive years on different makes of motorcycle (Yamaha and Honda) before unexpectedly switching to a Cagiva for 1991.

After his retirement from motorcycle racing, Lawson raced Indy Light cars, moving to IndyCars in 1996. His final motorcycle race was the Suzuka Eight-hour race in 1994 where he finished fourth on a Yamaha. In an interview with Dean Adams in 1993 Lawson said this of his time with Kawasaki: 'I have a lot of great memories from my Kawasaki days, they really treated me well the three years that I was there, fantastic really.'

AMA SUPERBIKE RACING 1983

Eddie Lawson departed for Europe but fortunately for Kawasaki they had Wayne Rainey to fill his place. A 21-year-old Californian, Rainey had proved the find of 1982 and like Lawson had graduated through dirt track racing in Shell Thuett's Yamaha team. Chuck Larsen (then head of Kawasaki Motors Corporation) groomed Rainey from 1979 for road racing, this continuing under the tutorship of Keith Code on a stock KZ750. When Rainey won the 250cc National at Loudon during 1981 on one of Lawson's KR250s, he earned a factory ride for 1982. For 1983, veteran racer Wes Cooley was hired to assist Rainey, Cooley fronting at the Daytona Formula 1 race on an Endurance-style Moriwaki-built aluminium-framed KZ1000-based racer. This had a linkage rear suspension and the mechanical anti-dive of the KR500, but Cooley crashed out of the 200-miler. He subsequently raced the ex-Lawson Z1000 Superbike in Formula 1 commenting that it handled better than the Endurance-style machine, taking a victory at Sears Point.

New AMA Superbike regulations for 1983 saw the maximum engine displacement at 750cc and Kawasaki were initially slow in developing their Uni-Trak GPz750-based Superbike. Honda had their well-developed VF750 and after Daytona, where Rainey finished a

distant fourth, the prospects looked bleak for another Kawasaki victory in the Championship. The GPz750 was still an air-cooled four-cylinder with two valves per cylinder and an older design, so a real David and Goliath battle transpired. The Honda juggernaut included two full factory machines, and Honda won the first six races of the series. However, after Mike Baldwin crashed at Pocono, Rainey, on the Steve and Mark Johnson-prepared GPz750-based Superbike won six of the eight remaining races. Against the odds, Rainey's exceptional riding and determination had given Kawasaki another AMA Superbike Championship.

Many of the problems with the GPz750 early in the season were caused through more radical camshafts. Although these delivered a 5bhp increase they also broke the valve springs, but by Brainerd the use of an improved valve spring material saw the Kawasaki as the equal of the Honda. Vance and Hines prepared Rainey's cylinder heads while Muzzy worked on Cooley's. As the 66.4mm KHI pistons were very high domed the KHI sand-cast cylinder heads used twin spark plugs per cylinder. Chassis development included longer 38mm racing forks and a new rear suspension linkage. Kawasaki then announced that, due to financial problems, they wouldn't be fielding a team in 1984. Rainey was left to pursue other fields, and like his predecessor, Lawson would prove his exceptionally ability on the world stage. Rainey won three 500cc World Championships and 24 Grands Prix before crashing at Misano in 1993, breaking his spine.

1983

For the last year of the Endurance World Championship run as a 1,000cc class the Z1000J again formed the basis of the factory Endurance racers, which was now the RZX1000. While the 998cc engine was much as before, with dual spark plug ignition and four Keihin CR carburettors, the powerband was wider. There were more developments to the chassis, the double loop frame now being rectangular section tubular aluminium. To add extra stiffening there were bolt-on diagonal braces running from the top tube to the bottom of the front loop. Although the machine was considerably more compact than the previous year and the short wheelbase contributed to agility, two steering dampers were required to provide stability for the 172kg racer.

Kawasaki again fielded two teams and started the season strongly with a victory in the Le Mans 24-hour race. Cornu, Gérard Coudrey and Pellandini won, with Lafond, Igoa, and Bolle second. Cornu and Coudrey then won the Eight-hour at the Nürburgring followed by Lafond and Igoa at the Österreichring. Cornu then teamed with Didier de Radigues and Thierry Espié to win the Liège 24-hour race. The Bol d'Or was a non-championship round and the works Kawasakis used 1,100cc engines in practice. However, in the race they reverted to the 998cc versions, both these retiring with piston failure. For the final event at Mugello, Cornu (with Jean-Louis Battistini) won with Lafond and Igoa second, but it wasn't enough to win the Endurance World Championship. However, Kawasaki again took the manufacturer's, championship in that final season for the Z1000-based racers.

NK-1 ROADRACING

Although not generally based on the older air-cooled fours, the machines created for the Japanese NK-1 (naked) series closely resembled the monster AMA Superbikes of the early 1980s. Created in 1994 to cater for the Japanese passion for American nostalgia, the NK-1 class has continued to grow. Most NK-1 Kawasakis were ZRX1100s and ZRX1200s, developed to produce around 160bhp and fitted with Superbike-spec wheels, brakes and suspension.

One of the most popular forms of racing in Japan, the NK-1 class, recalls the Superbike racing of the early 1980s with naked modern Superbikes based on the liquid-cooled ZRX1100 and ZRX1200 engines. *(Australian Motorcycle News)*

5 WORLD CHAMPIONSHIP SUCCESS

Baldé and Mang lining up for the 250cc Grand Prix at Silverstone in 1982. Mang came second and Baldé won the 350cc race. *(Mick Woollett)*

By far the most successful of all two-stroke road-racing Kawasakis were the KR250 and KR350 tandem twins of 1975–82. After initial disappointment these magnificent motorcycles were developed into virtually unbeatable Grand Prix machines. In the hands of Mick Grant, Kork Ballington, Gregg Hansford, Anton Mang, Jean-François Baldé, Hervé Guilleux and Edi Stöllinger they amassed a total of 73 Grand Prix victories, with Ballington and Mang taking eight World Championships between them.

Although an early prototype was exhibited at the Amsterdam show in 1970, Nagato Sato designed the KR250 during 1974, reverting to the earlier feature of rotary intake valves. With rotary valves the peak power was similar to that of a piston-port design, but there was considerable gain across the powerband. To overcome the problem of engine width that had disadvantaged the A1 and A7-R, Sato arranged the aluminium-coated cylinders in line, offset 16mm to the left to allow for the overlap of the steel inlet discs. Without a carburettor port in the back cylinder wall there was more space provided for the three transfer ports, also allowing the unbridged exhaust port to be wider. The bore and stroke were nearly square at 54x54.4mm, the longer stroke also seeing piston speeds increase beyond 4,000 feet per minute, considerably increased over the conservative 3,500 feet per minute previously adopted by Kawasaki engineers. The pistons featured a single ring and each

cylinder had a separate crankshaft, with the front running backwards and the rear forwards, ensuring both pistons thrust against the exhaust side of the cylinder for better crankcase sealing. These were geared to a seven-speed gearbox as allowed by AMA racing in the United States. Two gearboxes were available, a close-ratio or wide-ratio, driven through a dry multi-plate aluminium clutch from the rear crankshaft. One of these was peculiar for Daytona, the sixth gear used to fight the wind on one side of the banking and another gear to allow more rpm with the wind behind on the other side. Also driven from the rear crank was the water pump through a skew gear. The front crankshaft drove the Kokusan ignition, and the early engines had magnesium crankcases. Magnesium was also used for the crankcase covers, and twin Mikuni 32mm carburettors. These were positioned on the left, angled slightly upwards and feeding through straight inlet ports. With a 7.5:1 compression ratio, the power was around 50bhp at 12,000rpm, and in 1975 the KR250 was the most advanced 250cc motorcycle in existence. It was reputed that only 12 early examples were produced.

Because the two crankshafts were phased at 180°, with a 100 per cent balance factor, even with rubber engine mounts the early KR250s suffered from excessive vibration. The large engine speed horizontal vibration at mid-stroke also contributed to the expansion chamber header pipes breaking. The frame was a miniature duplex version of the KR750 and the running gear featured a single front disc brake, with the brake caliper cast into the fork leg, this either on the right or left. There were 36mm Kawasaki forks, and seven-spoke Morris magnesium wheels. Where the KR250 was superior to the competition was in the claimed weight of only 98kg, considerably less than either the Yamaha TZ250 or Aermacchi Harley-Davidson.

The first appearance of the KR250 was at Daytona in March 1975, ridden by Yvon DuHamel and Ron Pierce (standing in for an injured Jim Evans). Although Pierce (who had ridden all the competitive 250s) rated the Kawasaki as potentially the superior machine in its class, both he and DuHamel suffered ignition problems. In early 1975, five KR250s were also sent to England for Stan Shenton's Boyer-Kawasaki team. These were the same seven-speed models that went to the USA, but to allow them to comply with FIM regulations they had the seventh ratio rendered inoperative through a revised shifter drum. Thus for British short circuits, most of the ratios were unsuitable, the excessive vibration also contributing to failure of the main gear between the two crankshafts.

Opposite: An early KR250 as raced by Murray Sayle in Australia during 1976. *(Australian Motorcycle News)*

In its Grand Prix debut at Assen in 1975, DuHamel rode to a promising fifth place. (Two Wheels)

However, after the disappointment at Daytona Team Boyer was instructed not to race their KR250s until modified parts or a new machine were supplied. This arrived a week before the TT, but Grant could only complete one lap before the machine overheated.

After the TT, the KR250s were entered in the Dutch Grand Prix at Assen, where DuHamel rode alongside Team Boyer. DuHamel came fifth in the 250cc race, but Grant retired with brake problems. Although the KR250 lacked speed this was a very encouraging result. In the USA, development of the KR250 continued with Ron Pierce and tuner Steve Johnson. Johnson had previously worked on Phil Read's Yamahas and, to overcome cooling problems, a KR750 radiator was substituted.

Just before the Swedish Grand Prix in July the KR250 was withdrawn from Grand Prix racing, although they were allowed to race at British international meetings. DuHamel then returned to the USA where he rode the KR250 at Laguna Seca, but was slowed by brake problems. However, a third and fourth place in the Lightweight race was encouraging and enough to convince the Japanese to persevere with the project. By Ontario, Johnson had managed to increase the power to 52bhp with a safe rev ceiling of 12,000rpm, and KR250s were provided for DuHamel, Grant and Takao Abe. KR250s won both heat races and DuHamel was leading until his frame broke, leaving Grant to finish third.

While Shenton's machines lay stagnant during 1976, in the USA and Australia the KR250 was still raced. At Daytona, Pierce fronted with his machine prepared by Kevin Cameron, and both Nixon and Hansford also had KR250s. In the Lightweight international race, brake problems troubled both Pierce and Nixon, while Hansford suffered a failed big-end. Pierce eventually crashed after coolant leaked on his rear tyre while in fourth. By Loudon, in June, the two KR250s had a form of monoshock rear suspension with a single Monroe air shock absorber on one side of the triangulated swingarm. This provided room for the rear cylinder exhaust to be routed straight back, and while engine development was at a standstill, DuHamel still rode to an impressive second place in the Lightweight final. Although all three US riders (DuHamel, Nixon and Pierce) had KR250s for Laguna Seca, development of the KR750 had taken precedence and none finished. Results were a little better at Riverside where DuHamel finished third.

Apart from the improved engine there was also a revised frame for 1977, this featuring a Uni-Trak rear suspension system. Here are the KR250s at the West German Grand Prix where Kiyohara very nearly won. *(Australian Motorcycle News)*

1977

At Daytona in early 1977, Gregg Hansford and Murray Sayle turned up with new, and vastly improved, KR250s. During 1976, Sato had redesigned the engine and this was debuted at the Japanese Grand Prix at the end of 1976, Takeo Abe coming second to a works Yamaha. Within the engine the two crankshafts were now phased at 360°, cancelling the forces at mid-stroke, overcoming the earlier vibration, and giving a wider spread of power (from 6,000rpm). A new low-drag Kokusan ignition system fired both spark plugs simultaneously. Another change was to the rotary valves, the previous steel type now being thicker fibre (1mm) with less drag. Flame-sprayed aluminium valve covers replaced the wear-prone magnesium, and with 34mm carburettors, the power was now around 55bhp at 12,500rpm. A six-speed gearbox was standardised, but the most important development was to the chassis. Designed by Kinuo (Cowboy) Hiramatsu, the basic duplex cradle was conventional, although lighter and smaller than before, with a Uni-Trak monoshock rear suspension. The swingarm was constructed of steel tubing with a bellcrank providing a 2:1 leverage ratio on the upright Koni shock absorber. The swingarm also featured a lower brace and the rear axle rode on eccentric adjusters. There was a single front disc, the twin-piston Kawasaki caliper no longer cast in the leg of the still skinny 36mm fork. Hiramatsu also designed the fairing, the front being angled to generate downthrust on the front wheel at high speed. All this development saw the weight increase to 104kg, but this was still lighter than the competition.

Barry Ditchburn struggled with the new KR250 during 1977 but came third in the Nations Grand Prix at Imola.
(Barry Ditchburn)

Murray Sayle leading Rick Perry demonstrates the spectacular agility of the KR250 at Hume Weir in Australia during 1977.
(Australian Motorcycle News)

Kork Ballington was not only one of Kawasaki's greatest champions, he was amongst the most loyal. Nearly all his racing achievements were on Kawasakis.

(Mick Woollett)

KORK BALLINGTON

Hugh Neville 'Kork' Ballington's association with Kawasaki began in 1970 with one of the first production H1s. Born in Salisbury, Rhodesia on 10 April 1951, he moved to Pietermaritzburg in the Province of Natal, South Africa, at the age of 16. Ballington started riding motorcycles at the age of 14, obtaining a competition licence in 1967 when he raced a C110 Honda. Later, he successfully raced a YF1 50cc Yamaha and a CB175 Honda before his brother Dozy purchased an H1 500cc. Kork went on to win the Natal 500cc Production Championship in 1971 after which he

acquired a well-used H1-R from the Kawasaki importer. Ballington won the 1972 South African Unlimited Championship then obtained a Seeley frame. Installing the tired H1-R engine in the Seeley frame saw Ballington win a ticket to Europe after victory on its first outing.

His first sponsors in England, Aldridges of Bedford, recognised his ability and determination, as did Stan Shenton after Ballington managed fourth in the 1974 British Superbike Championship on the Seeley-Kawasaki (now with an H2 engine). 'That was a good bike and very competitive. Dozy breathed on the cylinders and heads and the motor retained all road parts except for the H1-R gearbox, dry clutch and H1-R carburettors. A set of expansion chambers to Kevin Cameron specs completed the "special". I used to give the works Suzukis and Kawasakis a run for their money on occasions' says Ballington. This led to his ride on the Team Boyer Kawasaki H2-R in the Thruxton 400-mile race. However, it wasn't until the 1978 season that Ballington received a works Kawasaki contract, mostly due to his performances on a Sid Griffiths Yamaha, and in particular, his victory in the 250cc and 350cc events at the 1977 British Grand Prix. Stan Shenton approached Ballington after a meeting at Brands Hatch towards the end of the 1977 British season, and he fronted the 1978 Grand Prix season on the KR250 and 350 in a team alongside Kawasaki veteran Mick Grant. His performances gradually improved and by the end of 1978 the combination of Kork and his brother Dozy as tuner were virtually unbeatable.

When Kawasaki retired from racing Ballington quit the European scene and during 1984 raced only the Suzuka Eight-hour race (on a GPz750 with Rob Phillis). For 1986 and 1987 he rode Hondas for Bob MacLean in the USA finishing second in the 1987 AMA 250 Championship and winning at Daytona. There were more representations on Kawasakis at Suzuka with Phillis in 1987 and 1988 (where he finished sixth) but that year he retired from racing. Ballington had won 31 Grands Prix and four World Championships, and was one of the most skilled and consummate champions ever.

In 1992, Ballington became a consultant to Kawasaki and an adviser on the X-09 project with the intention of fielding a full Grand Prix effort during 1993. 'Although I never had any managerial aspirations to run a GP or any other team, I would have grasped the opportunity to help Kawasaki with a comeback to GP racing with the X-09. It was unfortunate that the bike wasn't competitive and the project dropped at the end of 1992,' Kork Ballington told the author. He moved to Queensland, Australia in 1998 to devote more time to his family and began a fasteners business near Brisbane. Dozy also retired from motorcycles in 1987 to work on the Isle of Man.

In the 100-mile race Hansford ran out of fuel while lying third, his aluminium fuel tank only holding 20 litres instead of the claimed 22 litres. Sayle finished ninth, and Kawasaki was encouraged to contest the first European 250cc Grand Prix of the season at Hockenheim. They brought Akihiro Kiyohara from Japan and it was initially decided that Ditchburn would represent the British team until June, after which Grant would assist. At Hockenheim, Kiyohara qualified fastest, with Ditchburn third, while in the race, Kiyohara finished a close second and Ditchburn tenth. With only 0.1 second separating Kiyohara from Christian Sarron the new KR250 almost won a Grand Prix at its first outing. A week later at Imola, Ditchburn came third and in Spain he looked like winning until he crashed on a piece of Perspex lying on the track. Grant joined the Kawasaki line-up for the French Grand Prix with Ditchburn qualifying fastest. Ditchburn now felt he was under some pressure to perform, and suffering from food poisoning, crashed early on. Then it was to the Isle of Man where Grant rode the KR250 in the Junior TT, but retired with carburettor trouble.

Masahiro Wada replaced Kiyohara at Yugoslavia, but both Ditchburn and Wada struggled for form. Mick Grant joined Ditchburn and Wada at the next round at Assen, Grant riding to an easy victory, his first Grand Prix win, with Ditchburn third. At the Swedish TT Grant, the fastest in practice, rode to his second Grand Prix victory. At this stage of the season the Japanese contingent seemed homesick and returned to Japan, seemingly losing interest in the World Championship. This left the British team endeavouring to sort out the intricacies of the temperamental rotary-valve twins by themselves, and results suffered. Although Grant finished second in Finland, neither of the British KR250s finished at Silverstone. It had been a season of promise, but the hope of any World Championship disappeared when the Japanese technicians returned to Akashi.

In September, Hansford took his KR250 to Laguna Seca and gave the little Kawasaki its first major victory in America. There, he just headed Gary Nixon home in one of the best Lightweight races ever seen at Laguna Seca. In Australia and New Zealand too, Hansford had considerable success on the KR250, even managing an unlimited class victory in the New Zealand Marlboro series after his KR750 damaged a crankshaft.

1978

There was a new KR250 and a larger KR350 for the 1978 Grand Prix season, and a more concerted effort to win the World Championship in both categories. Engine developments extended to smaller, steel-caged needle roller bearings replacing the left-side brass-caged ball main bearings, and there was an aluminium box-section swingarm along with a more aerodynamic seat unit. The swingarm retained the Uni-Trak linkage, and the chrome-molybdenum tubular frame and non-adjustable forks were also unchanged. The KR350 was very similar to the KR250, a bore increase to 64mm giving 349.9cc. The clutch was strengthened, and the carburettor size increased to a Mikuni VM36SS. The claimed power rose to 75bhp at 11,800rpm, but with many shared components, the crankshaft and main bearing were more of a problem on the 350.

Although Stan Shenton remained team manager, Ken Suzuki coordinated the Team Kawasaki-Life UK effort, with Kork Ballington and Mick Grant as riders. In addition to the UK team there was also Hansford on the Neville Doyle-tuned Team Kawasaki Australia entry, and Anton Mang with a Sepp Schlögl-tuned KR250. Schlögl was an ex-Dieter Braun mechanic and came with vast two-stroke racing experience. The talents of the respective tuners, Dozy (Deryck) Ballington, Neville Doyle and Schlögl, were almost as important as the abilities of the riders, as correct carburetion on the disc-valve twins was critical. Kork Ballington told the author: 'without Dozy I may only have won two World Championships instead of four. He had the amazing ability to identify and eradicate problems before they could manifest themselves into DNFs, which he did with regularity on both KRs, particularly the temperamental 350. It was also amazing that he never had access to or used a dyno and yet on the rare occasions that he did get out the port grinders, never threw a cylinder away.'

At Daytona, Hansford rode the 1977 KR250 (now with twin front disc brakes), but as always his size penalised him, negating any weight or speed advantage of the KR250. As Neville Doyle says, 'because Gregg weighed 12½ stone he needed an extra five horsepower.' Initially they had trouble matching the pace of the

Top: For 1978, there was also the KR350, but the larger version wasn't as reliable as the 250cc. The 350cc always retained monoblock cylinders. *(Australian Motorcycle News)*

Opposite: Ballington came fourth in the opening 350cc Grand Prix of 1978 at Venezuela, and initially had some trouble adjusting to the Kawasakis. He went on to easily win the 350cc World Championship, and narrowly took the 250cc Championship as well. *(Mick Woollett)*

Bottom: The side-mounted Mikuni carburettors were also larger on the 350cc but the two versions were almost identical. *(Australian Motorcycle News)*

Yamahas, but a new ignition system restored the KR250's speed. Despite gear changing problems, Hansford won the Lightweight race. Mang, on a 1978 specification machine, came second.

Although an outsider in his first Grand Prix season, Hansford immediately showed the speed of the KR350 at Venezuela where he retired after a gearbox seal failed while he was leading comfortably. Hansford was initially refused a ride in Spain because he wasn't a graded FIM rider, but went on to win with the 1977 KR250. Undoubtedly, Doyle's and Hansford's experience with both the KR250 and Michelin tyres was an advantage earlier in the season. 'We started with a new machine and Hansford was much faster at the beginning,' says Ballington. 'The rear suspension system and the feel of the bike were so different from the cantilever rear-suspension Yamahas I rode during 1976 and 1977 that I had to learn to ride it and get the suspension working. We then had to improve the carburetion that was a long way off optimum out of the crate. We were also disadvantaged as Dunlop only had treaded front tyres at that stage.' Despite these problems Ballington easily won in Austria on the 350, its first Grand Prix win in only its second GP outing. Hansford was still suffering from his F 750 crash at Brands Hatch and Grant crashed, breaking his foot. In France, Hansford took a double victory, the 250cc race, again on the proven 1977 KR250.

The big break for Ballington came at the Nations Grand Prix at Mugello. 'In the first three rounds of the 250 Championship I was well and truly blown off by Gregg and Kenny Roberts on the factory Yamaha, but we quickly identified the problem areas and set about rectifying them. By Mugello I had come to grips with how the KR250 needed to be ridden, we started getting better power throughout the range and Dunlop came up trumps with a new construction and compound rear tyre which proved a match for the Michelins. They also now provided a good front slick which enabled me to brake as late as Gregg and enter bends with the front brake on harder than was possible on the treaded front tyre. I then simply rode my heart out!' says Ballington, and he narrowly beat Hansford in both races. At the next event, at Assen, after choosing the wrong tyres for a wet 250cc race, Ballington won the 350cc Grand Prix. By this stage in the season any tyre or speed advantage enjoyed

earlier by Hansford was eliminated and the disadvantage of his size on the small Kawasakis again became apparent. However, with the Swedish TT moved to Karlskoga, a bumpy circuit that no one had previously ridden on, Hansford found himself back in front with two comfortable victories over Ballington.

In Finland, Ballington won both races and Sepp Schlögl finally came to terms with the KR250. Mang finished fourth, a harbinger of things to come. No one really expected Mang to win at Silverstone after Ballington's ignition failed, but he narrowly took his first 250cc Grand Prix victory from Tom Herron. After a difficult season, Mick Grant came fourth, and Hansford crashed in an attempt to overcome his miserable start. In the 350cc race, Ballington sealed his first World Championship with an easy victory while Grant came third. All season, the 350cc had been more problematic than the 250cc. 'The 250 was a beauty,' Ballington told the author, 'but the crankshaft flapped so much on the 350 that it sometimes hit the crankcases. This led to the main bearing cracking, but Dozy came up with a solution by modifying the crankshaft dowel pin to allow the bearing to move with the crank. He was directly responsible for the success of the 350. As it was, the 350 ate crankshafts so quickly that we started every race with a brand-new (never run) crankshaft.'

Hansford got away to another bad start at the Nürburgring, allowing Ballington to comfortably win the 250cc GP. With a better start in the 350cc race though, Hansford took the lead before his throttle stuck. There was no doubt that the poor starts were disadvantaging Hansford in his chase for the 250cc title. At Brno, he was last away but rode through the field to be in second place at the end of the second lap, but he couldn't match Ballington's speed along the straights. The 250cc World Championship was decided at Yugoslavia where Ballington needed to finish only sixth to take the title. There, Hansford found the new circuit suited his style and, despite another poor start, rode away to win the 250cc race from Mang. Ballington's third place gave him his second World Championship, but only by six points. In the 350cc Grand Prix Hansford rode away for an easy victory after Ballington's KR350 went on to one cylinder, its first mechanical failure of the season.

1978 GRAND PRIX VICTORIES

250cc and 350cc World Champion: **Kork Ballington**

Spain (Jaráma)	250	**Gregg Hansford**
Austria (Salzburgring)	350	**Kork Ballington**
France (Nogaro)	250, 350	**Gregg Hansford**
Nations (Mugello)	250, 350	**Kork Ballington**
Dutch (Assen)	350	**Kork Ballington**
Sweden (Karlskoga)	250, 350	**Gregg Hansford**
Finland (Imatra)	250, 350	**Kork Ballington**
Britain (Silverstone)	250	**Anton Mang**
	350	**Kork Ballington**
Germany (Nürburgring)	250	**Kork Ballington**
Czechoslovakia (Brno)	250, 350	**Kork Ballington**
Yugoslavia (Rijeka)	250, 350	**Gregg Hansford**

Opposite: Mick Grant had a very difficult season during 1978 on the KR250 and KR350. He is seen on the 250 at the Belgian Grand Prix, where he failed to finish. *(Mick Woollett)*

Below: Kork Ballington giving Gregg Hansford a ride back to the pits during 250cc practice at the Belgian Grand Prix at Spa. *(Mick Woollett)*

1979

At Daytona in March, Mike Baldwin fronted with a 1979 specification KR250, while Ballington and Mang raced their 1978 versions. This year the KR250 challenge fizzled, Ballington retiring with a failed thermostat and Baldwin with clutch problems. In the World Championships though the KRs were again dominant, apart from a brief challenge from Morbidelli. Graziano Rossi on the Morbidelli rotary-valve inline twin easily won at Yugoslavia, following this with resounding victories at the Dutch and Swedish GPs. Ballington's mechanics, brother Dozy and Stan Shenton's son Stuart, managed to extract both power and reliability from the little twins. 'Dozy came up with some remarkable cylinder, head and pipe modifications for the British GP at Silverstone.' says Ballington. 'He cut extra exhaust ports and changed the transfer port timings as well as changing the angle of the header pipes. These developments created a stronger powerband with a lower peak rpm and I took pole position using this motor, almost one second faster than the regular KR250 that I had been using. For the race we reverted to the standard KR as we had not yet clinched the Championship and could not risk a DNF on the relatively untried set-up. As it turned out I won the race and clinched the title, but would not have beaten Rossi if he hadn't fallen in the last lap. For the remainder of the season we used the Dozy-tuned motor which kept us up with the new found speed of the Morbidelli.'

Neville Doyle continued to struggle to adapt the small KRs to Hansford's stature and riding style, but again achieved some remarkable success. There were now many more KR250s and KR350s on the starting grid, with Mang, Ditchburn, Estrosi, Stöllinger and Baldé also riding in various races. Slightly different rear-seat streamlining distinguished the machines from the previous year, and with the 350 crankshaft problems largely overcome, developments included 'pork chop' crank counterweights rather than a full disc type. Because the circuits at that time still featured long straights most KR250s used a single steel KR750 front disc and twin piston caliper.

Ballington soon found the form that had given him

Top: Gregg Hansford worked hard with the KR250 during 1979, but his size always penalised him. This is Hansford at the 1979 250cc German Grand Prix where he finished sixth. *(Australian Motorcycle News)*

Bottom: Ballington lining up for the 1979 250cc British Grand Prix at Silverstone. He went on to win the race, also sealing the 250cc World Championship. *(Mick Woollett)*

Hansford's 1979 KR250, as restored by Neville Doyle.

(Greg McBean/Two Wheels)

Krauser initially sponsored Toni Mang during 1980 and his Sepp Schlögl-developed KR250 surprised everyone with its speed. This is Mang in action at the Dutch TT where he finished third, but he went on to take the 250cc World Championship.
(Mick Woollett)

ANTON MANG

Born in Inning am Ammersee in Bavaria, on 29 September 1949, Anton (Toni) Mang was almost a veteran when he won his first World Championship, at the age of 31. His first motorcycle, a DKW RD 125 came when he was only 11 years old, but initially, it was skiing that appealed to the young Toni Mang. By the time he was 16 he was a Junior European ski-bob champion and he subsequently entered motorcycle racing with a 50cc Kreidler. A toolmaker by trade, he joined up with childhood friend and schoolmate, Sepp Schlögl, and Alfons Zender to create the completely homebuilt SMZ (Schlögl-Mang-Zender) 250cc. Like Schlögl, Mang also worked as a mechanic for former World Champion Dieter Braun, this leading Mang to a Yamaha TZ350 ride in the German Grand Prix of 1974. In 1975, Mang won the German Championship, moving into the World Championships in 1976 on a private Morbidelli. He came fifth in the 125cc class in 1976, winning the German Grand Prix, and in 1977 endeavoured to campaign both the 125 and a Suzuki RGB500. Hired by the German Kawasaki importer to ride the KR250 and KR350 for 1978, Mang's career then exhibited gradual improvement through until the late

1980s, although he didn't demonstrate he was superior to Ballington in any of their direct confrontations.

Life after Kawasaki's withdrawal from Grand Prix racing was initially difficult for Mang. Prior to the 1983 season he suffered a serious skiing accident and although he had a works 500cc Suzuki he missed more than half the season because he couldn't sit on a motorcycle. In 1984, Mang won only one Grand Prix, on a Yamaha, but with a Honda contract for 1985 he was back in contention for the 250cc World Championship with three victories. Mang then surprised everyone by winning his fifth World Championship in 1987, at the age of 38. This year he was undeniably the fastest and most consistent 250cc rider in the world. Then a slow recovery from a broken collarbone sustained at the first corner of the 1988 Yugoslavia Grand Prix prompted his retirement from Grand Prix racing. As Germany's most successful ever motorcycle racer, Toni Mang won 44 Grands Prix and five World Championships, spanning a decade. He was, and still is, revered as a hero by German fans, and was always flocked by crowds, especially in races in the Eastern bloc.

double championships the previous year. While he suffered a slight mid-season slump and had more breakdowns this year, after Finland, Ballington totally dominated the 250cc class. The 350cc Championship didn't come quite as easily as the Yamahas provided more of a challenge. 'One of the problems with the 350 was the powerband was a little narrow,' claims Ballington, 'probably because the stroke was too short in relation to the bore. During the season the factory supplied new porting and pipes in an effort to stay ahead. The difference between the 250 and 350 was like chalk and cheese. The 250 had a wide, strong powerband, was very smooth and handled like a lady whereas the 350, basically a 250 with too much horsepower, had a narrow vicious powerband, vibrated badly and with the same frame and tyres as the 250, was a bad-mannered and exciting ride indeed!' Hansford also had a poor start to the season, and it wasn't until the Nations Grand Prix that he found form. There, a change to twin Brembo front brakes (on both the KR250 and KR350) and Dunlop tyres for Yugoslavia improved his performance. Even though he was plainly more comfortable in his second European season, on most occasions Hansford couldn't match Ballington. During 1979, Ballington managed to find the perfect combination of speed and consistency and completely demoralised the opposition. He had the 250cc title wrapped up by Silverstone, and cemented his dominance with victories in the final two races. Even the 350cc Championship was sealed before the season's end. Again, Hansford finished runner up in the 250cc class and third in the 350cc. He was undoubtedly looking forward to the new 500 for 1980.

Barry Ditchburn's season on the KR250 was less memorable. Provided with one 250 and one 350, he struggled to get the temperamental machines running satisfactorily and refused to ride them at the British Grand Prix. It was only when he received one of Ballington's spare engines for the final two rounds of the British 250cc Championship at Oulton Park and Brands Hatch that he felt comfortable with their performance. He did however, win some international 250cc and 350cc races at Donington and Brands Hatch earlier in the season.

1979 GRAND PRIX VICTORIES

250cc and 350cc World Champion: Kork Ballington

Austria (Salzburgring)	350	**Kork Ballington**
Germany (Hockenheim)	250	**Kork Ballington**
Nations (Imola)	250	**Kork Ballington**
	350	**Gregg Hansford**
Spain (Jaráma)	250, 350	**Kork Ballington**
Yugoslavia (Rijeka)	350	**Kork Ballington**
Dutch (Assen)	350	**Gregg Hansford**
Belgium (Spa)	250	**Edi Stöllinger**
Finland (Imatra)	250	**Kork Ballington**
	350	**Gregg Hansford**
Britain (Silverstone)	250, 350	**Kork Ballington**
Czechoslovakia (Brno)	250, 350	**Kork Ballington**
France	250	**Kork Ballington**

1980 GRAND PRIX VICTORIES

250cc World Champion: Anton Mang

Nations (Misano)	250	**Anton Mang**
Spain (Jaráma)	250	**Kork Ballington**
France (Paul Ricard)	250	**Kork Ballington**
Yugoslavia (Rijeka)	250	**Anton Mang**
Belgium (Zolder)	250	**Anton Mang**
Finland (Imatra)	250	**Kork Ballington**
Britain (Silverstone)	250	**Kork Ballington**
	350	**Anton Mang**
Czechoslovakia (Brno)	250, 350	**Anton Mang**
Germany (Nürburgring)	250	**Kork Ballington**

1980

With the introduction of the KR500 and the trouble over the ill-fated World Series, Hansford missed nearly all the 1980 season and didn't contest any Grands Prix until the final round in Germany. Ballington also forwent the 350cc category to concentrate on the 500, and to make his life easier in the 250 GPs he had a new KR250. This now had separate cylinders and heads, with aluminium crankcases, and new five-port cylinders similar to those developed by Dozy Ballington. The three exhaust ports included two small exhaust ports next to one larger one and provided a broader spread of power. Compared with 1979, the Kawasaki presence was considerably less, with Toni Mang and Baldé alongside Ballington as the main contenders. Edi Stöllinger and Jean-Louis Guignabodet also rode KR250s and KR350s, but achieved only moderate results.

Mang too had individual cylinders for his KR250, but Sepp Schlögl developed these independently. At the start of the 1980 season, Kawasaki Germany withdrew their support leaving Mang with only Krauser sponsorship. With virtually no spares, many components were specially constructed, including the crankshaft and primary drive, and wind tunnel-developed fairing. With Kawasaki Germany unsure as to the competitiveness of the now three-year-old twins, Mang's machines had Krauser livery, and no 'Kawasaki' identification. 'We developed this machine together with Krauser who was our main sponsor,' says Toni Mang. 'Although the 250 was considerably developed our KR350 was almost standard.' The 350 also retained the earlier one-piece cylinder block.

Demonstrating the effectiveness of his revised KR250, Mang led most of the Daytona 100-mile Lightweight race before losing a slipstreaming battle on the final lap and finishing third. Mang then went to the Nations Grand Prix where he showed that his machine was more than a match for Ballington's, even though he was still coming to terms with the switch to Dunlop tyres from Michelin. Mang won the 250cc race (Baldé came second and Ballington crashed in a fluid spill along with Lavado and Marchetti, after setting the fastest lap of the race), but the Kawasaki domination of the 350cc class seemed to collapse without Ballington.

At the Spanish Grand Prix, Mang knew that Ballington would be unbeatable and settled for second, with an identical result in France. However, Ballington was surprised by the speed of Mang's machine. 'At the start of the season his KR250 was faster than ours,' he says, 'and we were not in a position to find more power because developing the 500 took precedence.' Kawasaki then took on ex-British Champion Martin Carney to assist in the development of the 250. Kork's luck then changed. An infected intestine resulted in a stomach operation and he missed three Grands Prix, leaving the door open for Mang to consolidate his grip on the 250cc title. By Assen, Mang had also come to an agreement with Kawasaki Germany to run with a 'Kawasaki' logo on the fuel tank, although the machines were still in the white Krauser colours. 'We had long discussions with Kawasaki to come to this agreement,' says Mang.

When Ballington returned for Finland he responded with a resounding 250cc victory but Mang's second place gave him his first World Championship. 'I feel I could have won the championship that year but I missed the Yugoslavian, Dutch and Belgian rounds. These were relatively safe circuits that I would have been prepared to stick my neck out at and not have held back as I did at Czechoslovakia.' says Ballington. With the 250cc title sewn up, Mang then set his sights on the 350cc Championship, promptly winning at Silverstone. Mang though, had no answer to Ballington who rode with customary masterfulness in the 250cc race. It was a Mang double at Czechoslovakia, KR250s filling the first three places. At the Nürburgring Ballington led a Kawasaki whitewash in the 250cc Grand Prix, but Mang lost the 350cc race (and the World Championship) to Jon Ekerold on the final lap.

The KR250's dominance continued in the USA where Eddie Lawson won the AMA 250 Expert Lightweight National Championship on the ex-Baldwin machine tuned by Steve Johnson. This 1979 specification KR250 still featured monoblock cylinders but Johnson went to considerable lengths to get the weight down to around 90kg. One of Ballington's KR250s was also supplied to Chas Mortimer for the Isle of Man Junior TT, but he failed to finish.

Ballington and Mang fighting it out at Paul Ricard in the 250cc race. Ballington then missed three events and with it any hope of retaining his title.
(*Australian Motorcycle News*)

1981

After blitzing the AMA 250cc Expert Lightweight Championship in 1980, Eddie Lawson fronted at Daytona on his Steve Johnson-tuned KR250 alongside World Champion Anton Mang. Lawson's bike now featured final drive by toothed rubber belt and Mang, now with Kawasaki sponsorship, was forced by the AMA to use Goodyear tyres. Mang finished a distant third while Lawson won the International Lightweight race. Mang had a new chassis that he tested but was dissatisfied with it. 'I tried it at Daytona but it was terrible,' Mang told the author. This new chassis included a tri-angulated swingarm and revised rear suspension linkage with a short connecting link to the rocker arm, similar to the KR500. Also tested during 1980 by Ballington (he found it acceptable but didn't race it), the geometry was altered slightly in the adaptation to the 1981 machine.

Unfortunately for Mang, he only had the new specification machines available for the opening Grand Prix at Argentina and his performances suffered as a result. Baldé though, provided with similar machines, realised the problem during early season tests at Paul Ricard and went to Argentina with the 1981 engines in the older frames. The superiority of the older set-up was evident by Baldé's win in the 250cc race and second place in the 350cc. Reverting to the earlier rear suspension design for the Austrian Grand Prix, Mang was immediately on the pace again and he won both Grands Prix in Germany. As in the previous season, Mang and his engineer Sepp Schlögl developed their own cylinders, pistons, crankshafts and exhaust pipes. There were also new carburettors and ignition this year although they retained the 1980 cylinders. Lawson also brought his early model KR250 (now with new cylinders) over from the USA for the German Grand Prix, but a main bearing failed on the third lap. Lawson also raced at Monza, where he crashed on the first lap after qualifying second, and crashed again in France. Mang soon settled into a flawless rhythm and was virtually unbeatable in both the 250cc and 350cc classes, sealing the 350cc Championship by the British Grand Prix and the 250cc Championship in Finland.

An impressive performance at the Isle of Man, where he set a new lap record of 109.22mph (175.73km/h) on one of Ballington's 1980 KR250s, saw Australian Graeme McGregor ride this again in the British 250cc Grand Prix where he finished a close third. Even though they were clearly dominant, Mang and Schlögl continued to experiment. They tried four-spoke magnesium wheels, built by PVM to their own design with streamlined spokes, to obtain additional speed. Unlike the 500s that were experimenting with 16-inch front wheels during this period, the Kawasakis retained 18-inch front wheels. This wasn't surprising as the KR chassis design was still essentially a developed design of an earlier period. However, outdated or not, by the end of the season Mang had won ten 250cc Grands Prix and five 350cc events. Baldé was second in the 250cc and third in the 350cc World Championships, further emphasising the excellence and dominance of the Kawasaki twins for the third successive year. Eddie Lawson too showed that the KR250 was more than a match for the new Yamaha TZ250H by winning the AMA Expert Lightweight National Championship for the second consecutive year.

Opposite: Toni Mang on his way to victory in the 1981 350cc British Grand Prix at Silverstone. The wheels were PVM, specifically designed with streamlined spokes.
(Mick Woollett)

Below: Eddie Lawson rode a few GPs during 1981 on the KR250, also going on to take his second AMA Lightweight Championship. Although an earlier specification machine the engine had individual cylinders. Other developments included a belt final drive.
(Australian Motorcycle News)

1981 GRAND PRIX VICTORIES

250cc and 350cc World Champion: Anton Mang

Location	cc	Rider
Argentina (Cuidad)	250	**Jean-François Baldé**
Germany (Hockenheim)	250, 350	**Anton Mang**
France (Paul Ricard)	250	**Anton Mang**
Spain (Jaráma)	250	**Anton Mang**
Yugoslavia (Rijeka)	350	**Anton Mang**
Dutch (Assen)	250, 350	**Anton Mang**
Belgium (Spa)	250	**Anton Mang**
San Marino (Imola)	250	**Anton Mang**
Britain (Silverstone)	250, 350	**Anton Mang**
Finland (Imatra)	250	**Anton Mang**
Sweden (Anderstorp)	250	**Anton Mang**
Czechoslovakia (Brno)	250, 350	**Anton Mang**

1982 GRAND PRIX VICTORIES

350cc World Champion: Anton Mang

Location	cc	Rider
France (Nogaro)	350	**Jean-François Baldé**
Nations (Misano)	250	**Anton Mang**
Dutch (Assen)	250	**Anton Mang**
	350	**Jean-François Baldé**
Belgium (Spa)	250	**Anton Mang**
Britain (Silverstone)	350	**Jean-François Baldé**
Finland (Imatra)	350	**Anton Mang**
San Marino (Mugello)	250	**Anton Mang**
Germany (Hockenheim)	250	**Anton Mang**

Opposite: By 1982, the KR250 was still much as it was several years earlier. Baldé's machine was essentially an updated 1979 version, but with individual cylinders. *(Two Wheels)*

Bottom: Although he narrowly lost the 250cc World Championship in 1982, Anton Mang was the final 350cc World Champion. *(Anton Mang)*

1982–83

Although Mang had proven totally dominant during 1981, by 1982 the little green racers were showing signs of age. They were virtually unchanged from 1980, yet the competition had progressed and there were not only Yamahas to contend with in the 250cc class, but also the 350cc Yamaha-based machines of Alain Chevalier. Baldé received more support this season, particularly from the French company Performance and he won the 350cc French Grand Prix after all the top non-French riders boycotted the event at Nogaro. It wasn't until the fifth Grand Prix that Mang notched his first victory, this occurring at Misano after he received a new-generation, wider Dunlop KR106 rear tyre. Baldé too showed he was much more competitive when he beat Mang in the Dutch 350cc Grand Prix, but his machines were now generally too slow.

Mang also had trouble setting up his Kawasaki for the triangular KR106 rear tyre and halfway through the season looked in danger of losing both championships. He was beaten again by Baldé at Silverstone and only won one 350cc event to eventually take the title for the second successive year. However, despite winning four 250cc Grands Prix he lost the Championship by one point to Jean-Louis Tournadre. Mang's 350cc World Championship coincided with the demise of the 350cc class, but both he and Baldé were convinced the KR250 would no longer be competitive in the 250cc class and were already looking for alternative machinery. With Kawasaki showing little inclination to design a new racer it was no surprise to see their official withdrawal

from Grand Prix racing at the end of 1982.

Although there was no official factory representation in Grands Prix during 1983, former Endurance racer Hervé Guilleux rented Baldé's KR250 from the Performance Team. Mechanic Francis Delcourt worked hard at keeping the KR250 competitive and Guilleux won in Spain, eventually finishing fourth in the 250cc World Championship. Developments included Mikuni 37mm cylindrical slide carburettors and, despite its age, the KR250 remained surprisingly competitive. By 1984, only Loris Reggiani was campaigning a KR250 in the World Championship. So came to an end the Grand Prix racing career of Kawasaki's tandem twin.

This lasted nearly ten years, five of which they dominated 250cc and 350cc Grand Prix racing. Considering they were supplied only to factory-supported riders (it was reputed 40 of the Uni-Trak model were produced) the results achieved by the KR250 and KR350 were truly staggering. Often there was limited factory development and they were sparsely represented on the starting grids. Undoubtedly much of the success of the KR250 and KR350 was due to the abilities of the riders and their respective engineers. The three rider/tuner combinations of Kork and Dozy Ballington, Mang and Schlögl, and Hansford and Doyle were amongst the finest in two-stroke racing history.

THE X-09

After making a modest return to racing with a four-stroke ZXR-7 during 1987 and 1988, Kawasaki produced another two-stroke 250cc Grand Prix machine during 1989, the X-09. Team Kawasaki Australia riders Aaron Slight and Michael Dowson tested this in Japan while they were competing in Japanese Superbike events, with the intention of competing in the World Championship during 1990. The X-09 then disappeared until two examples unexpectedly showed up at Daytona in March 1992. Kork Ballington managed the team, with South African rider Trevor Crookes teaming with Slight.

Veiled in secrecy, the machines were kept covered anytime they weren't out on the track, and the Japanese technicians only reluctantly allowed the AMA technical inspectors to see what was under the fairing. It transpired that the engine was an upside down V-twin, both cylinders pointing downward. A single downdraft dual throat carburettor valves fed directly into the crankcase through reed valves. Elongated oval bores aligned with the long axes of the reed cases, with intake flow passing through the flywheel separations. This was an intake system that seemed to entail a power penalty.

Ballington and Crookes spent considerable time testing and suggesting improvements throughout 1992, but according to Kork, 'the design was flawed and

without radical change was never going to produce the target power. Crookes was engaged to do test riding and I was there to help with chassis, tyre and suspension advice that my GP experience could assist.' The first outing was at Shah Alam in Malaysia at the end of 1991. There, progress was made with chassis settings, and a Japanese test rider turned in a lap that would have put the X-09 on the second row of the grid at the 250cc Grand Prix that had taken place there a few months earlier. This encouraged the factory to carry on with testing and development the following year. The engine configuration also caused significant exhaust problems with the exhaust exiting the rear and snaking around the engine. 'There were a lot of problems, one being with the KIPS (Kawasaki's power valve system) that they insisted on using,' Ballington goes on to say. 'The telemetry we were using told us that it wasn't benefiting the performance in any way except probably while pulling out of the pit lane. The engine would have performed better with controlled exhaust port timing as used on the faster 250s of the time. The other major problem was that the carburettor was in a rather hot spot. Lap times were usually best in cool weather, preferably with a high atmospheric pressure and on hot days it was notably down on power. Basically, the engine design was too radical a departure from what was proving to be successful in Grand Prix racing.'

While the X-09 was down on power, the chassis was excellent. 'There were two chassis,' says Ballington, 'the first as used at Shah Alam was too long but the second version, with revised geometry and a set of inverted front forks, worked well.' At Daytona, Slight retired while Crookes finished a respectable sixth after being in contention for third at one point. Crookes was then entered in the 1992 South African Grand Prix at Kyalami, but Kawasaki withdrew. The intention was to field a team in the 1993 World Championship but this didn't happen. In the words of Kork Ballington, 'My personal opinion is that by the end of 1992 Kawasaki realised the motor would have to be completely redesigned and I don't think the racing department would have been given the budget required. There also seemed to be no desire to continue.'

After a hiatus of nearly a decade Kawasaki made a tentative attempt to return to 250cc Grand Prix racing with the X-09 of 1992. This is the final version with upside down forks and a shorter chassis.
(Kork Ballington)

THE KR500

With the dominance of KR250 and KR350 in 250cc and 350cc Grands Prix it was no surprise to see Kawasaki move into the premier 500cc category with a four-cylinder 500, the KR500. Rumours had circulated since 1977, but it wasn't until 1979 that the competition department of six designers, three machinists and three fitters created the KR500. The first example ran in November 1979, and was shipped to England in early 1980, initially only for Kork Ballington. Expectations were modest with senior engineer Ichiro Tamura stating the intention was to prove reliability and gain respectable results in the first year. The engine layout was a square-four, with individual 54x54.4mm cylinders as on the 1980 KR250. Induction was by rotary valve, with four side-mounted Mikuni MV34SS carburettors, but despite the obvious similarity to the KR250 no engine parts were interchangeable. As with all Kawasaki racing two-strokes the cylinder bores were coated in chrome-molybdenum by a high-voltage electrofusion process to aid the retention of lubricating oil. Rather than magnesium, the engine castings were

aluminium, and there was the usual six-speed gearbox and multi-plate dry clutch, this employing eight friction and nine steel plates.

Hoping to capitalise on the revolution in frame and suspension design occurring at this period, Kawasaki went for a unique aluminium spine-frame monocoque design. The heavy gauge aluminium spine doubled as a fuel tank and supported the steering head as well as a rear extension carrying the engine mounts and swingarm pivot. Extra aluminium plates bolted to the tank and extended downward to support the outboard swingarm spindle. To some extent the engine was a stressed member, attached to the spine by square-section alloy tubes. Inclining the engine forward provided space for the near-vertical Kayaba shock absorber operated by an updated Uni-Trak system. This now featured a shorter strut connecting the triangulated aluminium swingarm with the rocker. The front suspension was by air-assisted telescopic forks and braking by twin, 290mm stainless steel Kawasaki discs and twin-piston calipers. At the rear was a 230mm drilled disc. The

In early 1980, Kawasaki unveiled the new four-cylinder KR500. From the left is Martin Carney, Seth Nagatomo, Dozy and Kork Ballington, Ichiro Tamura, Ken Suzuki, (not known) and Stuart Shenton. *(Two Wheels)*

wheels were generally 2.5x18-inch on the front and 4.00x18-inch on the rear, with Dunlop tyres. According to Kork Ballington, 'The KR500 was about 40 pounds too heavy and the wheelbase six inches too long. But the motor was fantastic, with really competitive horse-power.'

After a slow start, Ballington's 1980 season was further interrupted following his stomach operation, but he returned to achieve fifth in Finland. Generally though, the KR500 suffered handling and tyre problems. 'The tyres just couldn't handle the weight,' says Ballington. The Kayaba rear suspension unit also over-heated, and to overcome this Dozy and Stuart Shenton fitted ducts under the fairing to flow air to the shock absorber. Although he only earned points from three races, Ballington finished the season in 12th position.

Hansford was also earmarked for a KR500 ride but confusion over the establishment of the breakaway World Series prior to the 1980 Grand Prix season hurt Hansford more than any other rider. Loyalty to other riders saw him left with a Kawasaki contract that enabled him to race in only the final Grand Prix in Germany. There, he retired after his steering damper broke.

There was considerable development of the KR500 during the off season, ostensibly aimed at saving weight. The thinner-gauge aluminium monocoque frame was claimed to be lighter, with more weight saved through magnesium engine castings, wheel spacers, and brake calipers. According to Kork Ballington 'the 1981 ver-sion was slightly lighter but still too heavy and long.' As the engine was already powerful enough develop-ments were aimed at improving the mid-range torque. There was a mechanical anti-dive rather than the hydraulic system favoured by Suzuki with two rods con-necting the front brake caliper mounts to the bottom triple clamp. A new fairing provided improved aero-dynamics with a reduction in overall height. Early versions featured an enclosed aerodynamic front mud-guard, but to avoid potential controversy this was later cut down. Hansford tested the machine in Australia prior to the European season, and he qualified fastest at the Imola 200 in April before crashing and breaking his leg.

Early performances confirmed an improvement over 1980. Ballington finished sixth at Austria and qualified an impressive fourth at Paul Ricard. After successfully testing a 16-inch front wheel at Donington, this appeared at Assen to help compensate for the long, 58in (1,473mm) wheelbase. The long wheelbase was theo-retically an attempt to keep the front end down under power and the back end down while braking, but it lim-ited manoeuvrability and required higher lean angles. Hansford too was back from injury, and while neither rider was particularly happy with the handling, Ballington still gave the KR500 its best result so far with a third place. Hansford broke his leg again at Spa, ending his motorcycle racing career.

A double win at Snetterton in the British Superbike Championship provided Ballington with a much-need-ed morale boost. Kawasaki supplied a shorter swingarm for the British Grand Prix at Silverstone which reduced

Hansford astride one of his two KR500s at the Dutch TT in 1981. Coming back from injury he could only manage 14th and a crash at the next Grand Prix ended his motorcycle racing career. (Mick Woollett)

Unlike other Grand Prix motorcycles, the KR500 featured an aluminium monocoque chassis with the fuel tank incorporating the spine. This is Hansford's 1980 machine which he raced in only one Grand Prix. (Two Wheels)

There was a new KR500 for 1981, still with an aluminium monocoque frame, but the machine remained long and heavy. There was also a mechanical anti-dive system. (Two Wheels)

the wheelbase by about 1½in (38mm), and Ballington responded by setting the fastest lap in the race before retiring with disc valve failure. 'The shorter swingarm was something that I had asked for from the beginning of the season. This was steadfastly refused until just prior to Silverstone when a surprise package arrived from Japan. The effect was astounding and the bike came alive. Long bikes drift easily but drifting heats up the rear tyre which compounds the traction problem. The shorter bike allowed quicker cornering speeds without drifting and the rear tyre stayed at a workable temperature, so we gained on both fronts.' Ballington earned one more podium (a third in Finland), and a fourth in Sweden, to finish eighth overall in the 500cc World Championship. He had more success in the British *Motor Cycle News* Superbike and 500cc Championship, finishing second in both.

For 1982, Eddie Lawson was provided with a long chassis 1981-specification KR500 to race in the US Formula 1 series. He led the Daytona 200 for 28 laps but in other races, despite a second place at Elkhart Lake, was outpaced by the big-budget FWS Honda of Mike Baldwin. While Lawson persevered with the older model, there was a new KR500 for Ballington in 1982. The frame was now a welded plate spine construction, and the steering head was bolted to a slimmer spine with a separate fuel tank. Unfortunately, this resulted in an even heavier structure, placing more demands on the tyres. The forks and shock absorber were now Showa and the frame provided alteration of the steering head angle through tapered plates with eccentric adjusters at the bottom of the fork legs to adjust the trail. The mechanical anti-dive was retained but changed into a more complicated set-up of linkages which allowed the rider to choose the amount of dive he required by lengthening or shortening the top linkage arm. Despite being asked at the end of 1981 to allow for the use of incoming 17-inch wheels, as well as the existing 18-inch wheels, Hiramatsu went for the smallest possible frontal area and designed the bike to take only a 16-inch front wheel. It was impossible to fit anything larger, severely handicapping the team as Dunlop were then concentrating development on 17-inch tyres. Ballington struggled even more than he had in 1981. While it was easier to ride with a smaller rear tyre, Dunlop produced a new-generation KR106 eight-inch wide tyre

that Ballington preferred as it gave more grip. Dozy and Stuart Shenton managed to unleash even more power towards the end of 1982 when they separated the ignition trigger wires. 'Prior to this it had been hard to tune but there was now a lot more mid-range and bottom-end power,' says Ballington. 'It started popping wheelies all over the place and appeared to me to be the most powerful of all the 500s in straight line performance comparisons. Despite its shortcomings the chassis was a technical masterpiece and, considering there were no electronic exhaust port duration controlling devices as used by other teams, the engine was impressive. It was very commendable that Kawasaki had come within a whisker of producing a world beater in such a short space of time having started from scratch while the opposition had many years under their belts. Had the bike weighed the same as the opposition's it would have been truly formidable,' Ballington told the author.

Unfortunately, with too small a development budget the KR500 was left behind. Ballington went on to say, 'The change to Showa was another mysterious move that set the team back a year. Showa were contracted to Honda so the units supplied to Kawasaki were obsolete. By the end of 1981 we had the Kayaba units working very well and I was astounded when the 1982 KR500 arrived with Showa suspension. We were left with no internal parts and no time to get them working. It wasn't until the Spanish GP that Showa agreed to modify the suspension and this made a huge difference.' While Ballington finished eighth in Argentina, he retired in Austria. With revised suspension his performance improved at Misano, where he finished sixth, and he consistently managed a top ten finish, but this hardly did his ability justice. Ballington finished ninth in the 1982 500cc World Championship but had a more successful season in Britain. With six victories he easily won the British 500cc Championship and the ITV Superbike Championship. While the KR500 had not made much of an impact on the world stage at least Ballington left the British racing scene on a high note. When Kawasaki withdrew from Grand Prix racing at the end of 1982 that was also the end for the KR500. 'This wasn't unexpected,' comments Ballington, 'it was always conceived as a three-year project.' His 1982 KR500 now resides in his collection of Kawasaki racing machinery in Australia.

Opposite: Kork Ballington on his way to seventh place in the 1982 500cc Dutch TT. On this third version of the KR500 Ballington won the British 500cc Championship and very nearly won the British Grand Prix, but for brake problems.

(Mick Woollett)

6 ENDURANCE RACING RETURN

Terry Rymer and Carl Fogarty won the 1992 Endurance World Championship on the Kawasaki France ZXR-7. This Formula 1 machine was quite similar to Vieira's 1991 version. *(Australian Motorcycle News)*

Following Kawasaki's withdrawal from official competition at the end of 1983 there was only sporadic representation in Endurance races over the next few years. Not only were there the financial considerations of racing through this period of economic difficulty, but Kawasaki also didn't have a competitive 750. Their only suitable 750 was the GPz750R, this basically being a GPz900R with a 748cc (70x48.6mm) engine. The liquid-cooled 16-valve engine produced adequate power but the machine was large and heavy. Despite these drawbacks, for the 1984 Suzuka Eight-hour race there were several factory Moriwaki GPz750 entries. On one of these Kork Ballington teamed with Rob Phillis, but they retired after 15 laps. Kawasaki France continued to support Endurance racing during 1984, and at the Liège race in August entered a GPz750-based racer. They then fielded three GPz750s at the Bol d'Or in September but without success. The most surprising result for the heavy GPz750R though was Mile Pajic's victory in the 1984 World TT Formula 1 race at Zolder, on a private entry.

During 1985, Kawasaki France persevered with the Endurance racing GPz750R, this being unsuccessfully ridden by Jean Monnin, Roger Sibille and Christian Berthod. It wasn't until 1987 that Kawasaki made a cautious return to Endurance racing, with the GPX750R, designed from the ground up as a 750. Still a six-speed liquid-cooled four-valve four-cylinder double overhead camshaft design, this featured a central chain camshaft drive and no counterbalancing system. The 748cc engine had a smaller bore and longer stroke (68x51.8mm) and was 31mm narrower than that of the GPz750R. The cylinder head featured a valve train with individual rockers, the screw and locknut adjustment being positioned at the pivot end of the rocker. As the camshafts were closer together this provided a narrower included valve angle of 30°, and general weight saving saw a reduction of the engine weight by 17kg. All these developments contributed to an engine design more suitable for racing, and while the tubular steel street chassis would prove inadequate, this wasn't a problem in Endurance racing where freedom of chassis was allowed.

With Godier and Genoud back running the official Kawasaki Endurance team for Kawasaki France in April 1987, a semi-factory GPX750R was entered in the Le Mans 24-hour race. Pierre Etienne Samin, Pierre Bolle and Thierry Crine finished fourth. With strong finishes at the Österreichring, Spa and Jerez, the Belgian Johan van Vaerenbergh finished third in the 1987 Endurance World Championship. This was an encouraging sign for the factory, prompting them to provide two factory GPX750Rs for Kawasaki France at the Bol d'Or. The bikes were promising, initially leading the race before being sidelined by ignition failure. This led to the formation of Team Kawasaki, and the development of the ZXR-7 Endurance racer during 1988.

1988–90

Although the 1988 Endurance World Championship fell apart with the cancellation of several minor rounds, the three rounds, plus the Bol d'Or, still provided Kawasaki

with an opportunity to test their ZXR-7. At the first round, at Le Mans in April, Kawasaki France entered two GPX750R-based machines, with Jean-Louis Battistini, Bolle and Eric Delcamp finishing second. Endurance veteran Samin scrapped at the front early in the race but crashed. After the Suzuka Eight-hour race it was left to the Belgian team of Richard Hubin, Michel Simul and Michel Steven to uphold Kawasaki at the 24-hour race of Liège, where they finished third on a GPX750R. Then the ZXR-7s reappeared for the Bol d'Or, but both crashed out in the slippery conditions which were so bad that the race was stopped after 14½ hours.

The Endurance series lost its world championship status for 1989, the four-round series now being the FIM Endurance Cup. This year Kawasaki was more committed, not only entering the French team in the opening race at Le Mans, but also the Japanese trio of Sohwa, Tada and Shouichi Tsukamoto. With Honda also making more effort this year the factory ZXR-7s performed creditably, Patrick Igoa, Battistini and Bolle finishing second, with the Japanese team third. This instantly elevated the Japanese riders to the status of heroes in their home country. At the 24-hours of Liège only the French team raced. Their ZXR-7 ran out of fuel, and at the next event, the Bol d'Or, Christophe Bouheben destroyed the Endurance machine in a high speed crash. As part of its ongoing development the ZXR-7 was also raced in 1989 Japanese Formula 1 events, including the World Championship round at Sugo. There, Phillis finished fourth, later teaming with Aaron Slight to win the Arai 500 Endurance race at Oran Park on a factory ZXR-7 Formula 1 machine, with the TKA ZXR750 engine installed.

There were only three races in the 1990 FIM Endurance Cup, and Crine, Battistini and Delcamp led the Kawasaki challenge at the Le Mans 24-hour race in April. After losing time through electrical problems and a minor crash they finished fifth. Following Suzuka it was the Bol d'Or at Paul Ricard where the two factory ZXR-7s came second and third, Crine, Bolle and Battistini leading Morillas, Delcamp and Christian Lavielle. Again, the combination of Alex Vieira and the Honda RVF proved too strong.

THE SUZUKA EIGHT-HOUR RACE

Of all the Endurance events the most significant to the Japanese manufacturers has always been the Suzuka Eight-hour race. Unlike regular rounds of the Endurance Championship leading Grand Prix and Superbike riders are enlisted and the race pace is frenetic. Other factors too contribute to the uniqueness of the Suzuka race. Starting in daylight it ends in darkness, and often the Japanese factories produce special machinery.

Encouraging performances in the early 1987 Endurance races prompted Kawasaki to produce a new 750 for 'Good Luck Team Green' at the Suzuka Eight-hour. Their optimistic goal was to win the race so special ZXR-7 prototypes were provided for Kork Ballington and Robbie Phillis, as well as the Japanese pair of Takahiro Sohwa and Kiyokazu Tada. In accordance with FIM Endurance and Japanese F1 regulations, these featured production-based engines in a pure racing chassis. The twin-beam aluminium frame was a harbinger of the future, but all the factory machines retired, and it was Kawasaki France that achieved the best result, Samin and Crine finishing fifth.

The following year, Kawasaki again provided new ZXR-7s to Ballington and Phillis, Sohwa and Tada; as well as Samin

and Adrien Morillas, and Battistini and Delcamp. A month earlier, Sohwa had finished second in the World TT Formula 1 race at Sugo on the ZXR-7 so the factory knew they were competitive. These 150kg machines were hand-fabricated racers, producing around 130bhp at 11,500rpm with magnesium, 36mm Keihin carburettors. Braking was by new Nissin four-piston calipers. The aluminium frame would later form the basis for the production ZXR750H and on the prototype, the frame provided extremely quick steering, with 22.5° of rake and 3.5 inches of trail, although both this and the ride height were adjustable. The swingarm used eccentric adjusters and the wheelbase was a moderate 55.5 inches. The ZXR-7s ran strongly, Samin and Morillas finishing third, with Sohwa/Tada fifth and Ballington/Phillis sixth. Similar machines were entered in the 1989 event, Tsukamoto and Tadashi Maeda finishing fourth.

For the 1990 race there was a stronger entry but the results were disappointing. Phillis teamed with Michael Dowson, but the highest-placed ZXR-7 was the ninth of Japanese pair Sohwa and Tsukamoto. Results were better in 1991 when Keiichi Kitagawa and Ryuji Tsuruta finished fourth, and for the 1992 race there were updated Formula 1

Opposite: From 1988, Kawasaki entered special ZXR-7s in the Suzuka Eight-hour race, but good results eluded them. In 1990, the best finish was Sohwa and Tsukamoto in ninth. *(Two Wheels)*

Right: The ZXR-7s for the Suzuka race were always specially prepared and often Japanese riders achieved the best results. Keiichi Kitagawa and Ryuji Tsuruta finished fourth in 1991. *(Two Wheels)*

ZXR-7s. These had a new chassis with revised suspension and a ram-air induction system, and still weighed around 150kg, but performed disappointingly as most of the riders found them difficult to set up. Phillis and Slight eventually chose to race their ZXR750 Superbike, finishing sixth.

After trying for so many years to win this important race it all came together in 1993. In a field that included Eddie Lawson and Mick Doohan, Scott Russell and Aaron Slight triumphed on a revised ZXR-7, the final year for Formula 1. Three weeks prior to Suzuka the new ZXR-7 had taken the first three places in the Sugo round of the All-Japan F1 championship. Shoichi Tsukamoto went on to win the series from fellow ZXR-7 rider, Keiichi Kitagawa. The 1993 ZXR-7 had a lighter and stiffer frame placing more weight on the front wheel. The engine was a detuned Superbike example, placing a premium on fuel consumption but was significantly slower than the Yamaha and Honda. However, after qualifying third the ZXR-7 still won, despite being described by Scott Russell as 'absolutely the worst bike I have ever ridden. That particular bike just did not do anything I wanted it to, and it was never going to, that was clear.'

Russell was back in 1994, setting pole position on the works Superbike ZX-7R. Teamed with Terry Rymer, Russell almost won for the second successive year but lost to Honda-mounted Polen and Slight by a mere 0.28 second. The following year though Russell didn't race. Although this would have been his last time on a Kawasaki injuries sustained testing a Grand Prix Suzuki meant it was left to Anthony Gobert and Kitagawa to ride the Lucky Strike-sponsored Muzzy ZX-7R. They finished a distant 13th while Akira Yanagawa and Katsuaki Fujiwara upheld Kawasaki's honour by finishing third. Gobert was back on an updated Endurance specification ZX-7RR for the 1996 race, and teamed with Simon Crafar, came second. Completing a good event for the factory Kawasakis was the fourth place of Tsukamoto and Ryo, with Yanagawa and Shinya Takeishi fifth.

After the strong showing in 1996, four factory Kawasakis lined up for the 1997 Suzuka Eight-hour and in a wet and miserable race the best Kawasaki finish was Ryo and Takeishi's third place. At the 1998 Suzuka Eight-hour the Kawasakis were the first home behind the extremely strong Honda showing that year. Takeishi and Tamaki Serizawa came fourth, with Australians Damon Buckmaster and Martin Cragill fifth. There were even better results in 1999 and 2000. Yanagawa and Izutsu came third in 1999 and Peter Goddard and Serizawa third in 2000. In 2001, the ZX-7RR Superbike was outclassed, not only by the Honda SP1 but also by the new breed of Super Production machines, and the highest placed Kawasaki was the 11th of the Beet Motul ZX-9R.

Top: There were updated Formula 1 ZXR-7s for 1992, but most of the riders disliked them. Aaron Slight, teaming with Rob Phillis, finished sixth. *(Two Wheels)*

Middle: After six years of development Scott Russell and Aaron Slight won the 1993 Suzuka Eight-hour race, on the final version of Formula 1 ZXR-7. *(Two Wheels)*

Bottom: Anthony Gobert, teaming with Simon Crafar, came second on an updated Endurance specification ZX-7RR in 1996. *(Two Wheels)*

Opposite: Akira Yanagawa began his career with Kawasaki with a third place in the 1995 Suzuka Eight-hour race. *(Two Wheels)*

1991–94

After two years without world championship status, the FIM reinstated the Endurance World Championship for 1991, coinciding with a resurgence of Kawasaki's dominance in this category. Honda seemed to be caught unaware, allowing Kawasaki France to sign reigning champion, Portuguese-born Alex Vieira. The works Formula 1 ZXR-7 Endurance racers only needed to retain production crankcases, and with no weight limit were considerably more exotic than the ZXR750R Superbikes. They featured a different frame and bodywork, with a single ram-air intake, 43mm upside down Kayaba forks, and ISR front brakes.

Poor pit work and niggling problems ended Kawasaki's hopes of winning the opening rounds, but at Malaysia Vieira and Battistini won after Crine crashed his ZXR-7 while leading. With the cancellation of the British round at Donington Vieira needed to win the Bol d'Or, and this he did comfortably. Teaming with Miguel DuHamel and Battistini they dominated the race, despite stopping to replace the carburettors and ignition during the night. The final Endurance round was at Phillip Island and Rob Phillis teamed with Battistini to win the six-hour race. Vieira's second place gave him another Endurance title, Kawasaki's first since 1982.

The dominance of the ZXR-7 was even more evident in the 1992 World Endurance Championship. Again, Kawasaki France entered two teams, Christian Bourgeois signing three British riders alongside Alex Vieira. TT star Steve Hislop joined Vieira, with Terry Rymer and Carl Fogarty on the other ZXR-7. Rather than the established stars though it was Rymer and Fogarty who shone this year, especially in the 24-hour races that earned double points. Teaming with Michel Simul they easily won their first ever Endurance event, the Le Mans 24-hour race, after Vieira, Hislop, and Battistini retired. Then it was on to Spa where, despite clumsy pit stops and Fogarty breaking a finger after clipping a corner post, the British pair (this time with Jehan d'Orgeix) again crossed the line first.

The victorious ZXR-7 was still a 1991-spec machine but for the Suzuka Eight-hour the factory provided updated versions. After Suzuka it was back to Europe for the Bol d'Or where Rymer, Fogarty and Hislop again dominated,

leading the second factory ZXR-7 by five laps. Rymer and Fogarty now had an unassailable grip on the title and initially Kawasaki withdrew from the final two events in Australia and Malaysia. Only the threat of the withdrawal of world championship status saw Fogarty and Rymer entered for the final two rounds. They won both six-hour races easily, demonstrating their clear superiority.

The year 1993 was the final season for the World Endurance Championship to be run under Formula 1 regulations and, faced with increasing costs, the series struggled to maintain credibility. It didn't help that three races were cancelled, but still Kawasaki France fronted at Le Mans with two teams. There, Wilfrid Veille, Adrien Morillas and Brian Morrison won after the works Suzukis retired. There was only one factory ZXR-7 entered at the next round at Anderstorp, Morrison, Battistini and Veille taking an easy victory. Hoping to secure further easy points, the same team raced at Spa but failed to finish after a series of misfortunes. This time the privateer British Phase One ZXR750R of Steve Manley, Simon Buckmaster, and former *Cycle World* magazine associate editor Doug Toland triumphed. It was the first British privateer victory in ten years, and the first time an American had won a 24-hour world championship race. Scott Russell and Aaron Slight continued the Kawasaki dominance at Suzuka but it fell apart for Bourgeois at the Bol d'Or. Both the Kawasaki France ZXR-7s failed to finish, and it was Toland (this time riding a Honda) who won the championship.

With the 1994 Endurance World Championship run under Superbike rather than F1 regulations, the gap between the factory and privateer machines was narrowed. There were only four rounds and Kawasaki France fielded two ZX-7Rs at the Le Mans 24-hour race. Rymer, Morillas and Battistini cruised to a comfortable victory. Only one works Kawasaki was entered for the 24-hour race of Liège at Spa, Morillas, Battistini and Denis Bonoris winning easily. Then it was to Suzuka and the Bol d'Or where both the Kawasaki France entries suffered problems but Morillas's sixth place was enough to give him the title. The first Kawasaki home was the Phase One ZXR750R of Steve Manley, Robert Holden and Mike Edwards, which came second.

Opposite: Run under Superbike rather than F1 regulations for 1994, Adrien Morillas still managed to win the Championship for Kawasaki. Morillas is seen on his way to victory at the 24-hour race of Liège at Spa. *(Two Wheels)*

Below: Endurance racing is one of the most punishing forms of motorcycle competition, but the British pair of Fogarty and Rymer totally dominated the sport during 1992. Here they are, after winning the final race at Phillip Island. *(Australian Motorcycle News)*

1995–2001

Only Honda and Kawasaki had competitive factory Endurance racers for 1995 and the Kawasaki France entry of Rymer, Battistini and Jehan d'Orgeix started at Le Mans strongly until Battistini crashed when his front disc shattered. Electing to miss the Assen event, the next race was at Spa where the factory Kawasaki finished second. Victory finally came at the Bol d'Or, the Kawasaki France ZX-7R controlling the race to win by six laps. In a close finish to the Championship Rymer lost by a solitary point.

Although still popular with the crowds, by 1996 the factories were reluctant to commit full resources to the Endurance World Championship. Kawasaki France still ran the older ZX-7R, this proving good enough to win three rounds of the five-round series. Only one factory machine was entered for the opening round at Le Mans, and Piergiorgio Bontempi, D'Orgeix and Brian Morrison scraped home to give Kawasaki their fourth victory in five years in this event. As the next round at Assen conflicted with a World Superbike race Morrison teamed with Stéphane Coutelle and French journalist Bertrand Sebileau on the sole factory entry. Run over two eight-hour races on successive days the Kawasaki won by 11 laps, elevating Morrison to the lead in the Championship. He extended this further at the Spa 24-hour race with his third win in a row, this time teamed with Coutelle and Bontempi. As always the Suzuka Eight-hour race was really a separate event to the rest of the Endurance series, with none of the regular championship contenders figuring in the results, so it was on to the Bol d'Or. Two factory Kawasakis were entered, but Morrison's race ended when the ZX-7R's rear axle broke. Despite this misfortune Morrison had enough points to take the title.

With clearly the fastest machine, Kawasaki again expected to win the 1997 Endurance World Championship, but it was not to be. At Le Mans, Morrison again teamed with Bontempi and D'Orgeix, but mechanical failure sidelined their machine. Rymer replaced Bontempi for the Spa 24-hour race and the Kawasaki looked like winning until the engine blew up half an hour from the end. With two DNFs and the title now beyond reach, the Kawasaki finally held together at the Bol d'Or, Rymer, Morrison and D'Orgeix winning by just over a minute at a record-breaking pace.

At the Le Mans 24-hours, the opening round of the 1998 Endurance World Championship, Kawasaki got off to a good start when the semi-factory ZX-7RR of Sebileau, Thierry Paillot and Igor Jerman won, with the official Kawasaki France entry of Bontempi, Gregorio Lavilla and D'Orgeix second. Then it was to Spa where Iain MacPherson was drafted alongside Sebileau and D'Orgeix. They led until a broken chain and holed exhaust dropped them to second. None of the European regulars ventured to Suzuka so it was to the Bol d'Or where team manager Bourgeois hoped either Sebileau or D'Orgeix would seal the title. He split the riders but both machines retired, Sebileau's dropping a valve and D'Orgeix's holing a radiator. Sebileau finished third in the Championship.

By 1999, the status of the Endurance World Championship was considerably diminished. Despite huge crowds (120,000 for the Bol d'Or), the top GP and Superbike riders deserted the class and all the French-based factory teams chose only to contest selected events. Essentially the factory ZX-7RR was unchanged, although as with the World Superbike racers, engine developments included a new cylinder head, camshafts and exhausts. Again, the Le Mans 24-hour race was a Kawasaki benefit, Sebileau, Steve Hislop and Chris Walker teaming for victory. However, with the factory entry retiring at Spa, followed by a boycott of Oschersleben, the Championship slipped away. At the Oschersleben 24-hour race the Kawasaki Swiss entry of Herbert Graf, Martin Rieder and Christian Künzi was credited victory, but failure at the Bol d'Or ensured no Kawasaki riders figured in the final results.

With the Flammini Group involved in the promotion of the Endurance World Championship for 2000 there were now six events on the calendar. The French-based factory teams concentrated only on the two French and one Belgium venues so it was left to privateer teams to fight out for the Championship. Of these, the French GMT Kawasaki team was one of the most successful, Sébastien Scarnato, Nicholas Dussage, and Christophe Guyot winning the 24-hour

Opposite: Terry Rymer very nearly won the 1995 Endurance World Championship on the Kawasaki France ZX-7R, but had the consolation of winning the Bol d'Or. *(Two Wheels)*

race at Oschersleben. They went to the Bol d'Or with a chance of winning the Championship, and with some factory engine parts were leading until a con-rod broke after 14 hours. The official Kawasaki France team of Sebileau, Jerman and Ludovic Holon came second.

Further developments to the Endurance series for 2001 saw the introduction of a Super Production class, although the Endurance World Championship still went to the highest placed Superbike. The Superbikes were generally outclassed by the Super Production machines but the ageing ZX-7RR remained competitive against the other Superbikes. Representing Kawasaki this year was the Team Bolliger Switzerland ZX-7RR of Herbert Graf, Marcel Kellenberger and Anton Heller, but results were lean. As one of the stalwarts of the Endurance World Championship, Kawasaki's future involvement will depend on how the class develops and whether the Superbikes will survive the onslaught of the popular Super Production machines.

7 SUPERBIKE

One of Russell's most spectacular rides was at Daytona in 1995 where he won after crashing and remounting. *(Two Wheels)*

By 1987, not only was there an improvement in the general economic climate and worldwide motorcycle sales, but Kawasaki also had their new GPX750R. Although obviously designed as a budget street motorcycle, at least this could be adapted for competition. As always, the conflict between accountants and racing enthusiasts in the company predominated, but conditions now prevailed for a low-level return to competition. Not to be discounted either was the influence from distributors who wanted to see a return to racing, particularly those in Australia and France. Team Kawasaki Australia decided to develop a GPX750R and signed Len Willing and Rob Phillis to ride, Willing winning on the machine's debut in Tasmania in March 1987. Phillis won at Oran Park, eventually finishing second in the Australian 1,000cc Championship. He also finished second in the 1,000cc Australian Grand Prix at Winton. This was enough to prove to the accountants in Akashi that the GPX750R had potential.

ROBBIE PHILLIS

Hailing from the Australian country town of Wagga, Robert Allan Phillis was born on 27 April 1956. He learned to ride motorcycles on a Honda Supercup around Albury Airport where his father was a groundsman. Working as a carpet layer, Phillis found the time to indulge in dirt track and motocross, making the break to road racing in 1974 at the local Hume Weir circuit on his KX250 motocross bike. During 1976 he campaigned a Yamaha TZ350C, and by 1977 was one of the leading A-grade road racers in Australia. This led to a ride on a Kawasaki Z650C in the 1978 Castrol Six-hour Production race where he won the 750 class teaming with TKA rider Rick Perry.

After a successful period racing Suzuki Superbikes, winning the Australian Superbike Championship six times and culminating in a Grand Prix RGB500 test for Roberto Gallina at Misano, Phillis was signed by Team Kawasaki Australia. Initially this was to ride the GPz900R in Production racing, but it led to the Superbike ride in 1987. Prior to this Phillis had impressed on occasional TTF1 forays to Europe but like many colonials was ambivalent about racing outside Australia full-time. It was only with the guidance of mentor Peter Doyle (son of Neville) that Phillis eventually made the move to Europe. During 1988, a public appeal raised the money for Phillis to race in Austria and by 1990 he was the only rider officially representing Kawasaki in the World Superbike Championship. Despite finishing third during 1992 his contract wasn't renewed for 1993. As Phillis said to the author, 'it was the biggest kick in the guts I ever had in my career. Even today it really rankles, and I know that with both Polen and Roche out of it I could have won the Championship.'

Although offered a works Ducati ride by Raymond Roche, Phillis remained loyal to Kawasaki and stayed with TKA to contest the Australian Championship. As it transpired his final season in Australia was disappointing and he then rode for Kawasaki Germany in the German Pro Superbike Championship during 1994. Phillis returned to Australia in 1995 but was asked to join the Swiss-based Emil Weber Kawasaki team for 1996. 'Weber prepared the best and fastest Superbike I ever rode,' says Robbie. He still competed in various World Superbike races that year, but struggled to overcome injury and stay on the pace. 'Your judgement doesn't improve as you get older, and I was 42 when I retired in 1998,' he told the author. Phillis contested the 1997 German Pro Superbike Championship and was a regular top ten finisher. He had managed to make a living racing motorcycles for more than 20 years and always promised a job by Kawasaki, Phillis is currently Kawasaki Australia road race coordinator.

Above: Robbie Phillis led Kawasaki's return to Superbike racing during 1987 and 1988 on a GPX750R. This is Phillis with the Superbike and Production racer.
(Australian Motorcycle News)

Opposite: For 1989, Kawasaki released the ZXR750H1 and in the hands of Phillis was a more competitive Superbike. Phillis won the Australian 1,000cc title and performed creditably in some World Superbike events.
(Australian Motorcycle News)

1988

The year 1988 saw the establishment of the production-based World Superbike Championship and, while the GPX750R was considerably less exotic than Honda's new RC30 or Ducati's 851, Kawasaki cautiously entered the series under the auspices of Kawasaki France and Team Kawasaki Australia. Kawasaki France, entering machines for Adrien Morillas and Eric Delcamp, contested the European rounds, their GPX's prepared by Kawasaki Endurance stalwarts Georges Godier and Alain Genoud. They provided the first upset win of the season when, in front of 55,000 spectators at the Hungaroring, Morillas won the second race, beating Mertens's Bimota by a wheel. Bimota then ludicrously protested the legality of the GPX750R's seat but this was rightly overturned. While they achieved consistent top ten finishes it wasn't until Le Mans in September that Kawasaki France managed another podium. There, Delcamp came second in a rain-affected race.

On the other side of the world Rob Phillis rode the Team Kawasaki Australia GPX750R. Prepared by Peter Doyle with a customer racing kit, the GPX was the same machine raced during 1987. After making the trip to the Österreichring, Phillis rewarded Kawasaki with two sixth places at their home ground in Sugo, and consistent third and fourth places in Australia and New Zealand. Phillis also won the Australian 1,000cc Road Race and Endurance Championships that year. Considering the GPX750R was hampered both by the steel production chassis and standard carburettor rules these were outstanding results. The competition was strong too as he beat Yamaha-mounted, and future multiple World Champion, Mick Doohan on several occasions. Undoubtedly impressed by his achievement, KHI then supplied Phillis with a ZXR-7 Formula 1 machine for the annual Australian Swann Series. He convincingly beat Doohan and Michael Dowson at Oran Park, but crashed at the next round, breaking his hand.

1989

It was inevitable that the developments during 1987 and 1988 on the ZXR-7 Endurance and Formula 1 racer would find their way to the production line. In order to be more competitive in the World Superbike Championship Kawasaki needed a new 750, and for 1989 released the ZXR750 (ZX750H1). While the basic engine architecture was unchanged, the ZXR750 incorporated a number of performance improvements to assist the Superbike programme. There was a new cylinder head with the valve actuation by bucket tappets, allowing for steeper intake ports, but increasing the included valve angle slightly, to 33°. With the stock carburettor size ruling prevailing for World Superbike there were also larger (but not large enough) Keihin CVKD 36mm semi-downdraft carburettors, tilted at 45°. As on the ZXR-7, twin-snorkel tubes ducted fresh air from the fairing to the engine bay, but on the first ZXR750 this wasn't directed straight into the airbox. Used by all the distributor teams, the factory racing kit included larger (27.5mm inlet and 24mm exhaust) valves, 13:1 pistons, and increased the power to a claimed 140bhp.

With World Superbike regulations requiring a street chassis, the ZXR750 frame was patterned closely on that of the ZXR-7 prototype. In the interest of maximum rigidity the compact aluminium frame consisted of two 90x330mm extruded main beams connecting a cast alloy steering head to a hollow swingarm pivot structure. A top alloy rib, and an internal rib bisecting the main beams further improved rigidity. Alloy downtubes bolted to the main structure, doubling as engine mounts. While the frame was undeniably strong, it was also quite heavy at 16.5kg. The swingarm consisted of box-section aluminium extrusions and connected to a Uni-Trak suspension system through an eccentric pivot ride height adjuster. As it came out of the box the ZXR750 was also set-up for wide, 17-inch wheels front and rear, but was too heavy and suffered from slow steering and a long (1,455mm/57.28in) wheelbase. While certainly an improvement over the GPX750R, as the basis for a Superbike racer, it was still too street-orientated to be thoroughly competitive. Not only was there the Honda

1990

RC30 and Ducati to contend with, but there was also Yamaha's OW01.

KHI obviously sensed their ZXR750 wouldn't be as competitive as they had hoped and they still didn't field a fulltime factory team in the World Superbike Championship. It was again left to Kawasaki France to contest the opening European rounds but the ZXR750s lacked pace. With Endurance riders Patrick Igoa, Pierre Bolle and sometimes Christophe Bouheben (filling in for an injured Bolle), the Godier-prepared machines struggled to finish in the top ten. However, although there were still no special parts, Godier's development had yielded a 6bhp increase by Austria, along with a reduction in weight to the minimum of 165kg. This enabled Igoa to finish fifth in the second race at the Österreichring. It wasn't until Sugo though that the ZXR750 managed a rostrum finish, but it was in the hands of TKA rider Robbie Phillis with a third place. This prompted the factory to finally provide some special engine parts to the Godier team and, for the first time in the season, Igoa had the speed to qualify on the front row at Hockenheim. Unfortunately, these appeared too late to make an impression on the Championship as the final rounds were in Australasia, outside the realm of the Kawasaki France team.

For the Australian round at Oran Park the Kawasaki presence was considerably stronger, with Phillis joined by Sohwa and New Zealander Aaron Slight. Phillis rewarded the factory's faith by providing them with a second and third place. The team then went to Manfeild in New Zealand for the final round, Slight finishing second in race one. Although it had been a miserable season for Kawasaki, their new ZXR750 not managing to win a single race, Phillis finished 11th in the Championship while only competing in three rounds. Team Kawasaki Australia provided the ZXR750 its only championship with Phillis winning the Australian 1,000cc title, Slight coming second. It was enough to ensure Phillis and Team Kawasaki Australia represented the factory in World Superbike during 1990. The Phillis/Team Kawasaki Australia headed the factory effort for the next three years.

In response to the disappointing performance of the ZXR750H1 during 1989, there was an improved H2 model for 1990. This incorporated many features of the 1989 race kit, but more importantly for World Superbike there were larger intake ports with Keihin CVKD 38mm carburettors. Complementing these engine developments was a new frame (5kg lighter than before) and a new swingarm. The swingarm brace was eliminated, with more sheet metal used in the construction, and although the H2 was an improvement, it was still too long and heavy. In the hands of Scott Russell and Doug Chandler though the H2 was good enough to dominate the US AMA Supersport series, Chandler leading Russell in an easy win in the Daytona 750 Supersport race with Russell winning the Championship.

For this third year of the World Superbike Championship, with the sponsorship of Shin Etsu (noted for producing computer chips for the doomed Space Shuttle Challenger), KHI supported a one-rider team. A crew of 15 factory engineers and testers prepared the kitted ZXR750 with a host of factory parts before they were raced under the auspices of Team Kawasaki Australia. Team manager Peter Doyle set up base in Frankfurt and 33-year-old Phillis was contracted for the season. The ZXR750s had a higher compression ratio of 13.6:1, a factory titanium exhaust, and due to the larger homologated carburettors the power was increased. The airbox was also sealed to prevent hot air entering from the radiator. Most development though was aimed at improving the braking and handling. Phillis's machine featured upside down, 43mm Kayaba forks, a Kayaba shock absorber and six-piston Nissin front brake calipers, and was now close to the weight limit. Phillis also benefited with preferential treatment from Michelin, receiving 'A'-grade tyres. Despite the H2 model receiving a stronger swingarm, the factory ZXR750 swingarm featured additional welded sheet alloy bracing and weighed in at 167kg.

Phillis reckoned the 1990 ZXR was 6mph (11km/h) faster than the 1989 version and described the machine as 'really good'. He immediately impressed in the open-

Opposite: Phillis earned a full-time ride in World Superbike for the 1990 season on the improved H2 model, finishing fourth overall. *(Australian Motorcycle News)*

ing round at Jerez. Yet the weight disparity with the twins was still a problem for the Kawasaki and a bad crash at Hockenheim dented Phillis's confidence. It didn't help either that at Brainerd Doug Chandler gave Kawasaki their first win of the season. Despite having to revert to standard carburettors and being 10kg over-weight, Chandler's Muzzy ZX-7 was also noticeably quicker than the TKA ZXR750. Chandler was then invited to Sugo by Kawasaki where he repeated his Brainerd performance with the third place and a win. At the Malaysian round at Shah Alam, Sohwa and Dowson also rode ZXR750s, but it was Phillis who finally found form with two second-place finishes. He ended the season on a strong note with victories at Phillip Island and Manfeild, and fourth in the Championship.

AMA SUPERBIKE RACING 1989–95

After becoming the leading rider in the Muzzy squad from 1991, Scott Russell rode the ZXR-7 to victory in the 1992 AMA Superbike Championship. *(Cycle World)*

In the USA for 1989, Kawasaki fielded a factory-supported team for the first time in six years, Rob Muzzy coming back to Kawasaki after a stint with Honda. He signed 23-year-old Doug Chandler to ride a ZX-7, the US designation for the ZXR750. Chandler was the only salaried rider in the class but it took some time before Muzzy managed to make the ZX-7 competitive. AMA regulations allowed for a 1mm overbore, as well as the homologation of larger carburettors, but valve and oil leakage problems caused retirements. Muzzy

also experimented with alternative brakes and suspension including White Power upside down forks and Performance Machine brakes. By August most of the problems were overcome and the ZX-7 was fast and reliable. Chandler won the final two races at Lexington, Mid-Ohio and Heartland Park, Kansas, finishing fifth in the Championship.

For 1990, Scott Russell and former Daytona 200 winner John Ashmead joined Chandler on Muzzy Kawasakis. With the homologation of 40mm CV and Keihin flat-slide carburettors, Muzzy's incremental development saw his ZX-7s become the fastest in the world. Merlyn Plumlee tuned Chandler's machine while Russell's mechanic was Gary Medley, who would stay with Russell throughout his time with Kawasaki. The Muzzy machines retained the White Power forks and four-piston brakes, and with victories in New Hampshire, Road America, Miami and Mid-Ohio, Chandler was in a class of his own. He easily won the AMA National Championship Road Race (Superbike) series, and showing increasing improvement, Russell was third. The departure of Chandler to Europe saw Scott Russell assume the role of lead rider in the Muzzy team for 1991 and who was joined by Jacques Guenette Jnr. Russell, on the new ZX-7R, was clearly the fastest rider in the Championship, winning four Nationals: New Hampshire, Charlotte, Heartland Park and Texas. However, inconsistency saw him just fail to win the Championship.

With defending champion Thomas Stevens joining Russell, the 1992 Muzzy team was the strongest in the Championship and the season began well when Russell gave Kawasaki their first ever victory in the Daytona 200. In one of the closest finishes ever Russell beat Ducati-mounted Doug Polen by 0.182 seconds at an average speed of 110.669mph (178km/h). Russell did not have it all his own way, and while he only won two more Nationals (New Hampshire and Texas), he was clearly the fastest rider and deserved the Championship. Stevens finished second in the Championship, again emphasising the development by Muzzy. The ZXR-7s ran Keihin 41mm flat-slide carburettors, but even when entered in various World Superbike races (with stock carburettors), the Muzzy machines made more top-end horsepower. They also featured a different combination of cycle parts, with Performance Machine

spun aluminium wheels, 330mm front discs, and four-piston billet-brake calipers.

There were new AMA Superbike regulations for 1993, with absolute displacement limits enforced and more freedom regarding carburettors and front forks. To prevent extremely exotic components there was now a claiming rule. There was also a relaxation in connecting-rod material requirements, but at Daytona, the Muzzy Kawasakis used 140bhp 1992-spec engines with steel con-rods and valves in the interest of reliability. There, Russell was only narrowly beaten by Eddie Lawson, but with Russell concentrating on the World Superbike Championship Miguel DuHamel rode the Muzzy ZX-7R in all AMA Superbike rounds. Japanese rider Sohwa joined him but the most surprising Kawasaki performance came from Dale Quarterley. As a privateer with significant sponsorship Quarterley had access to Muzzy engines and won one National, at Mid-Ohio. He ended second in the Championship. DuHamel won at Sears Point to take third overall.

The 1994 season started strongly with Scott Russell winning his second Daytona 200 on the Muzzy ZXR-7. It was an impressive performance, Russell starting from 64th on the grid after suffering mechanical problems in his qualifying race. With Russell back in Europe defending his World Superbike title, Sohwa, former World Superbike Champion Fred Merkel, and Canadian Steve Crevier raced the Team Muzzy ZXR-7s in the AMA Championship. Sohwa rode consistently to finish third overall and Russell came back to win the final race at Road Atlanta.

There was no stopping Russell at Daytona in 1995. After qualifying fastest, he crashed on lap two, only to remount to take the lead and win the race in devastating style. It was Russell's only US ride that year and Pascal Picotte and Crevier rode the ageing ZX-7Rs in the rest of the AMA Championship. After a promising result at Pomona (where Crevier finished second) everything fell apart for the team. Dogged by mechanical problems and crashes, as well as being demoralised by Russell's defection to Suzuki, it wasn't until the end of the season that the Muzzy Kawasakis got back on the rostrum. By then it was too late and Picotte's sixth overall was the most disappointing result for Kawasaki since 1989. The new ZX-7RR was eagerly awaited for 1996.

1991

It was evident that KHI was serious about winning the World Superbike Championship as there was yet another new ZXR750, the ZX750J, for 1991. Not only was this was more suited to racing but a higher performance limited-production version, the ZXR750R (ZX750K) was also available. Central to the new 750 was a shorter stroke (71x47.3mm) engine, and on the ZXR750R there were larger Keihin KVKD 39mm flat-slide carburettors. The camchain was moved from the centre to the right, allowing the crank journals to be closer, there were five instead of six main bearings, and the crankshaft was 23mm

Phillis was again the sole factory rider in the 1991 World Superbike Championship, the improved 'K' model providing him with third in the Championship.

(Australian Motorcycle News)

1992

shorter. A new cylinder head design with a 20° included valve angle accompanied the shorter stroke, with a return to the single rocker per valve actuation system, and 28 per cent less reciprocating weight. Further reduction in internal friction was attained through a semi-dry sump.

With the 'K' model also came a new aluminium frame, constructed from welded aluminium sheet rather than extrusions. There were no bolt-on lower frame tubes and the engine was a stressed member, rigidly mounted in six positions. The result was a much more compact machine with a significantly shorter wheelbase of 1,420mm (55.9in). The ZX750K was a noticeable improvement over the H2, Scott Russell easily winning the 1991 AMA 750cc Supersport Championship.

In the World Superbike Championship the new ZXR750R was the only four-cylinder 750cc to consistently challenge the dominant Ducati 888 which still received a significant weight advantage. Although Phillis's ride was in doubt after Chandler won in Sugo, his two victories at the end of the 1990 season again saw him back as the sole factory rider, and still under the auspices of Team Kawasaki Australia. There was now no outside sponsor, and the factory ZXR750R was surprisingly competitive, straight out of the box. The engine was fitted with the usual race kit, but included a higher lift factory inlet camshaft and valve springs, along with special exhaust header pipes. The compression ratio was 13.2:1, with the power gradually increased to around 144bhp at 13,800rpm. Phillis was not too happy with the Kayaba suspension so TKA installed 42mm Öhlins upside down forks and a revised, more linear, rear suspension linkage with an Öhlins shock absorber. While Nissin six-piston brake calipers were used early in the season, disc warping saw experimentation with both ISR and Brembo brakes, the Brembo being favoured by the end of the season. There were also wider, 17-inch Marchesini rims (3.75 and 6.25 inches) for the Michelin tyres. While Phillis failed to win a race, by mid-season factory parts saw him a consistent rostrum finisher and he ended the year third in the Championship.

In an effort to break the Ducati stranglehold Kawasaki took a leaf out of the Italians' book by entering more factory ZXR750Rs. Aaron Slight joined Phillis in the Australian-run factory team, now sponsored by the Japanese transportation company Moving, and promptly won the season opener at Albacete, in Spain. Scott Russell and Takahiro Sohwa also fronted in the early races but Kawasaki's challenge fizzled after Russell returned to the USA and Slight was sent to Japan for Suzuka Eight-hour testing. By this stage, Phillis had won in Belgium and Andorra and was leading the Championship.

Still developed by Peter Doyle, with mechanics Dave

The 1992 ZXR750R undressed. The chassis was significantly improved this year and enabled Phillis and Slight to win three races.

(Australian Motorcycle News)

1993

'Radar' Cullen and Michael O'Rourke, the ZXR750R engine was largely unchanged from the end of 1991. The 1992 customer race kit included 1mm larger valves, a revised airbox, higher lift inlet camshafts, 2.5mm longer con-rods, and two-ring 13.5:1 pistons. There was also a new non-programmable CDI ignition with a different advance curve. Two different crankshafts were used, but Phillis generally didn't favour the very light version. There was considerable development of the airbox, this feeding air beneath the fairing nose with a deeper intake area. The power was 145bhp at 13,800rpm at the gearbox, new exhausts emphasising mid-range power, and two large radiators from the F1 bike kept the engine cool. The Formula 1 ZXR-7 engine was used for the rest of the year after the Suzuka Eight-hour race.

While the engine was largely unchanged from 1991, there was considerable development of the chassis. With the help of Öhlins technicians development centred on the rear suspension, now incorporating a new four-link system for the shock absorber. This raised the ride height by 10mm and gave more rear wheel travel. A by-product was increased front end bias and quicker steering, offset by increasing the trail to a massive 108mm. The frame had extra bracing at the front, and an adjustable swingarm pivot. Unlike other teams that were using carbon discs, Phillis used 320mm cast-iron Brembos. Still with Michelin tyres the wheel sizes were 3.50x17 and 5.75x17 inches.

The turning point in the Championship occurred at Mugello when Phillis crashed while dicing with Doug Polen and Giancarlo Falappa. Phillis claimed that Falappa had almost run him off the track at the previous chicane, prompting the risky braking move to make up time. Thus he lost the Championship lead to Polen and played catch-up for the rest of the season. In the words of Peter Doyle, 'Phillis fell in a bit of a hole mid-season but in the sense that the Ducati was a better bike, for me he was World Champion two years in a row.' The final straw for Phillis occurred at Monza when he learnt his contract wouldn't be renewed, despite having been told that if he finished third during 1992 he would be re-signed.

With the loss of Moving as an outside sponsor, there was considerable reorganisation of Kawasaki's racing activities for 1993. Shigeki Iwasaki headed the new Motorsports Department which united domestic and international racing programmes separately from the Engineering Department. The World Superbike team shifted from being under the auspices of Team Kawasaki Australia to that of Kawasaki Motors Corporation, with Scott Russell as the lead rider. The Australasian connection was retained with Peter Doyle as team manager and Aaron Slight seeing out the second year of his contract.

Although the ZXR750R was the most successful four-cylinder Superbike during 1992, further develop-

Rob Muzzy (left) and Peter Doyle ran the team that gave Scott Russell the 1993 World Superbike Championship.
(Australian Motorcycle News)

ment saw a new ZXR750R (ZX750M) for 1993, incorporating many features from the ZXR-7 Formula 1 machines. This included the single ram-air induction system feeding a larger airbox and a new frame with an additional steering head gusset, thicker main beams, and an extra cast section around the swingarm pivot. There was also more aerodynamic bodywork. The new chassis was significantly improved, as evident in early season Daytona testing when the entire Muzzy team favoured the production M chassis over the 1992 racing version.

The Superbike engines were no longer supplied by KHI and, with an updated customer kit and Muzzy exhaust pipe, the power was 150bhp at 13,800rpm. Compared with the earlier factory engines the power was biased strongly towards the top-end (8,500–14,000rpm),

Scott Russell on the new Muzzy ZX750R 'M' which he rode to victory in the 1993 World Superbike Championship. *(Two Wheels)*

Slight initially finding this difficult to adjust to. There was continual experimentation with camshafts and exhaust pipes to improve the power curve, along with titanium valves. More development concerned the chassis. Not only was the frame stronger, but the rear suspension linkage was similar to the final version used in 1992 by Slight and Phillis. The geometry was unchanged but there was now an adjustable swingarm pivot and the steering offset could be modified for each circuit. There were new Öhlins 46mm forks, and in an effort to overcome the disc warping of the previous three years, the front brakes were 290mm carbon with six-piston Nissin calipers. Now using Dunlop rather than Michelin tyres (on 3.75 and 6.25x17-inch Marvic wheels) the improvement over the 1992 version was dramatic. The only real problem was that the ZXR750R was a touch heavy at 167kg. According to Peter Doyle, 'with the factory stepping back we gained from Muzzy's engine development and they gained from our chassis knowledge. There was not one part of the chassis you would call a factory part, but Slight's chassis was five per cent better, and Scott's around 30 per cent improved over what he had in 1992.'

At the beginning of the season it was impossible to predict that the Championship would become a battle between Russell and Ducati's Carl Fogarty. Russell won at Hockenheim, but didn't lead the standings until after the sixth round at Brno. Then, at Sugo, the Muzzy Kawasakis were plainly down on speed compared with the wild card Japanese factory machines of Kitagawa and Tsukamoto. For the second race Russell received a factory engine with a new exhaust pipe that provided more mid-range power, and led home a top four Kawasaki benefit. This signalled a change in fortune for Russell. Although Slight beat him at Monza he went to Donington and won both races despite being injured from a practice crash. Leading the second race Slight reluctantly obeyed team orders and let Russell win. 'It would have been neither here nor there if I had won,' says Slight, 'I felt then it was time to move on.' When the final event in Mexico was cancelled Russell ended up World Superbike Champion by 29 points. Although he only won five races to Fogarty's 11, Russell was consistent and only crashed once, when Giancarlo Falappa hit him in Spain.

Distinguished by his 'Screaming Chief' helmet, and one of the most successful of all Kawasaki road racers, Scott Russell is also their most recent road-racing World Champion. (Australian Motorcycle News)

SCOTT RUSSELL

Born in College Park, Georgia, on 28 October 1964, Scott Russell had a Honda 50 from the age of five. His first racing bike was a 1974 Honda XR75 and he raced junior motocross from 1975 until 1977. 'Then I got bored. I was a kid, only 13 years old,' says Russell. His parents divorced while he was in high school. 'The family wasn't close and I dropped out of school in the 11th grade. I had to take care of things on my own somehow,' he says. At the age of 17 he was working in a plastic-bag factory and it wasn't until he was 19 that Russell even thought about motorcycles again, when he got a Kawasaki LTD440 cruiser. 'I rode that thing back and forth to work every day for a year or so then got a GPz750 and I was fast.' Russell then decided to go racing, his first year in novice club racing being 1986. After that his rise through WERA (Western/Eastern Roadracing Association) and Suzuki Cup races was meteoric. He turned Expert in 1987 and by 1988 was a professional racer. Russell raced in both AMA Superbike and Super Sport, finishing second in the 750 Super Sport class. He finished tenth in the AMA Superbike series and earned the Road Racing Rookie of the Year award.

This led to his first factory ride, a Yoshimura Suzuki, in 1989, and he won his first Superbike National (at Road Atlanta), eventually coming second in the Championship. 'Then Muzzy came along, offering me less money than Suzuki, but I took it because he had the best thing going at the time. With what Chandler was starting to do on the ZX-7

at the time I decided it was time to get on that,' says Scott.

When Russell left the Muzzy Superbike team midway during the 1995 season to fill Kevin Schwantz's spot in the Suzuki 500 GP team it led to an acrimonious end to his Kawasaki involvement and created considerable ill-feeling. Legal wrangling saw a compromise where Russell would ride in the Suzuka Eight-hour (although he missed this through injury), but ultimately Russell's career was hindered. By 1997 he was back in World Superbike on an uncompetitive Yamaha R7, those heady days where he was a World Superbike frontrunner seemingly far behind him. However, Russell could still perform, especially at Daytona, winning the 200 miler in 1997 and 1998. This was his fifth Daytona 200 victory, earning Russell the title 'Mr Daytona'. Then he rode for the Harley-Davidson Superbike team in 1999 and 2000, the VR1000 being totally uncompetitive. Russell signed with HMC Ducati for 2001 but suffered a badly broken leg in a crash on the starting grid at Daytona.

Despite a life punctuated by emotional misfortune, Russell exhibited extraordinary natural talent, focus and determination. His mother committed suicide after a long period of depression, and then he went out and won the Daytona 200. Earlier, a woman friend drowned in the bath at his house from convulsions brought on by cocaine. His career may have waned after he left Rob Muzzy's team but Scott Russell gave Kawasaki their only World Superbike Championship. He was also one of the most successful of all Kawasaki racers, with 14 World Superbike race wins, 11 AMA Superbike Nationals, and their only Suzuka Eight-hour victory.

1994

Following victory in the World Superbike Championship (although Kawasaki failed to win the constructors' title), the racing programme was now a full factory operation, with works bikes, Japanese-prepared engines, and a full-time Japanese engineer. The number of Japanese personnel involved always gauged the factory's seriousness and, at last, KHI were taking World Superbike racing seriously. Still under the auspices of Rob Muzzy, former Kawasaki tuner Steve Johnson managed the team while Peter Doyle resumed his duties with TKA in Australia.

There had been few changes to the ZXR750R. The engine was much as it was in 1991, but there were some slight combustion chamber developments and internal friction limited peak power to 155bhp at the gearbox. Rather than titanium valves, Muzzy preferred steel, and there was a new, fully sealed airbox and a pre-programmed ignition system. The regulation weight for four-cylinder Superbikes was reduced to 160kg, and the ZXR750R weighed in at 161kg. Generally, the chassis was the same as for 1993. The suspension was still Öhlins, with 46mm front forks, and the front brakes were carbon Nissin with six-piston calipers. This tried

and tested design was initially very successful, and the reduced weight differential between the twins and fours (now 15kg) undoubtedly helped the Kawasaki. Also, the two main competitors, Ducati and Honda, had all-new designs to sort out and Russell won four races at the start of the season. Then he crashed twice while testing, and with a stiffer chassis, encountered handling problems. Terry Rymer replaced Slight in the Muzzy team, but he had a miserable season and rarely finished in the top ten.

With all Kawasaki's hopes resting on Russell, he was provided a special factory bike for Sugo, winning both races. The engine had a gear camshaft drive and the frame was hand built to production specification, but it was returned to the factory after the race. Russell won again at Mugello and at Donington, where both races were in the rain. The Championship went down to the final event in Australia and there, former Team Kawasaki Australia motocross star Anthony Gobert rode Rymer's machine, setting pole position and winning the second race. Russell ended the year second in the Championship. Although he had won nine races it wasn't enough to beat Carl Fogarty in the overall standings.

Russell's 1994 ZXR750R was very similar to the Championship-winning 1993 version but it wasn't good enough to win for a second year. This was the last year for carbon front disc brakes.
(*Australian Motorcycle News*)

In addition to the World Superbike Championship, the ZXR750R was also a strong performer in Japan. This is Keiichi Kitagawa on his way to winning the opening round of the 1994 All-Japan Road Racing Championship. *(Australian Motorcycle News)*

600 SUPERSPORT RACING

Iain MacPherson has ridden the official Kawasaki Racing Team ZX-6R in the World Supersport Championship since 1999. Although he had a good season in 1999, the 2000 season was less satisfactory. (Ian Falloon)

The bourgeoning 600 Supersport class has been accepted with alacrity by all the Japanese manufacturers, although Kawasaki's interest has been spasmodic. They often haven't produced a suitable machine, but although the 1990 ZZ-R600 was more of a sport-touring motorcycle, it performed creditably in this highly competitive class. In the UK, John Reynolds won the 1990 British 600 Supersport Championship, and Scott Russell came a close second in the AMA Supersport series. It wasn't until the release of a revised ZZ-R600 (or ZX-6 in the USA) for 1993 that the Kawasaki was considered competitive, with Honda's CBR600F2. Surprising most pundits, Miguel DuHamel, on a Muzzy ZX-6, proved nearly unbeatable in the 1993 AMA 600 Supersport Championship.

The considerably more sporting ZX-6R appeared for 1995 and this proved ideally suited to the new 600cc Thunderbike Trophy run alongside Grands Prix. With three victories German Pro-Superbike Champion Udo Mark took the trophy on the Rubatto-Lortz ZX-6R. Yet it wasn't until 1996 that the ZX-6R broke the Honda domination in the USA when Mike Smith secured a victory at Laguna Seca, Thomas Stevens going on to take second in the Championship. In Australia that year, Kevin Curtain gave Kawasaki the 600 Supersport Championship. There was a new Ninja ZX-6R for 1998 that was not only more powerful, but also lighter and more nimble, and with six race wins Chandler came second in the 1998 AMA Supersport Championship. Damon Buckmaster and Andrew Pitt

The young Australian rider Andrew Pitt was the unexpected World Supersport Champion in 2001. *(Kawasaki Racing)*

were first and second in the Australian Supersport Championship that year.

Although the ZX-6R had proven itself at a national level, it wasn't until 1999 that there was an official Kawasaki Racing Team entry in the World Supersport series. Iain MacPherson, a 31-year-old Scotsman, rewarded the team with three race wins, and finishing second in the Championship. His ZX-6R was wonderfully prepared by Martin Gopp, who worked closely with Supersport race engineer Yamamoto-san. Andrew Pitt won the 1999 Australian Supersport Championship on a ZX-6R, then joined MacPherson in the Kawasaki Racing Team for 2000. For this year there was yet another new Ninja ZX-6R (ZX600J) – lighter and even more performance-orientated than before. However, despite the new machine neither MacPherson nor Pitt

were serious contenders for the title and the team only managed one rostrum finish. In the USA though, Eric Bostrom came close to taking the 2000 AMA Supersport Championship, winning two races.

There were no changes to the KRT World Supersport line-up for 2001, but with a racing kit as allowed by World Supersport regulations, the power was increased to around 114bhp at 13,000rpm. Pitt immediately showed how improved the machine was with several rostrum finishes, only narrowly missing a victory at Brands Hatch. Despite not winning a race earlier Pitt's consistency saw a surprise victory in the 2001 World Supersport Championship after arch rival Paolo Casoli crashed out in the final race at Imola. It ended a great year for the ZX-6R as this time, Eric Bostrom easily won the 2001 AMA Supersport Championship.

1995

This was the final year for the ZXR750R in its current form and there were few changes to the World Superbike racers. Altered regulations saw a ban on carbon brakes, with the minimum weight for four-cylinder machines being increased to 162kg to compensate. Most of the problems encountered by the Muzzy team centred on the supply of Dunlop tyres after an earthquake in Kobe in Japan where the racing tyres were manufactured. The late shipping of the new season's machines (after the Daytona 200 in March) also handicapped testing and there was also the mid-season loss of Scott Russell to the Grand Prix Suzuki team. Developments of the engine included a gear camshaft drive, titanium Pankl con-rods (still 2.5mm longer), and with a 13.5:1 compression ratio the power was 155bhp at 14,000rpm. There was experimentation with double exhausts (at Hockenheim) although most development was with the tyres, suspension and brakes. Öhlins suspension was retained, while the front brakes were 320mm steel with six-piston AP calipers. Unfortunately, something was lost in the balance of the machine and not only were they down on power, but they were difficult to ride, with lap times slower than in 1994. It was also obvious that the factory was more intent on developing the new 750 for 1996.

After his spectacular debut at Phillip Island, Anthony Gobert was signed to ride alongside Scott Russell in the Muzzy team, but there were also several privateer and distributor-backed teams. Often, Piergiorgio Bontempi, John Reynolds (on the Revé Racing ZXR750R), and Jochen Schmid achieved better results than the factory team. Struggling to overcome a lack of pre-season testing and adjustment to new circuits, Gobert consistently crashed in qualifying while Russell was preoccupied with other things. New minimum weight regulations (160kg for fours and only a 5kg differential with twins) coincided with the loss of Scott Russell and the Muzzy team's best early result was a sixth (Gobert) at Misano. It wasn't until Monza that new engines arrived, and at Salzburg Gobert was finally the fastest Kawasaki rider. He went on to win the first race at Laguna Seca, seemingly more motivated by Russell's departure. He won his second race of the year, the last at Phillip Island, to finish fourth in the Championship. Considering the difficulties experienced during the year it was an admirable result.

1996

In an effort to retain the Superbike titles they once possessed the development of the replacement ZXR750R was entrusted to Kawasaki's Racing Group. For the first time the design started life as a limited edition race-orientated model, the ZX-7RR (ZX750N), and a less compromised design for competition. Using the previous engine as a base, and with an ultimate target of 170bhp, there was a further reduction in the stroke, to 44.7mm, and a bore increase to 73mm. Combustion efficiency was improved through shorter, straighter intake ports and a direct shim and bucket valve actuation system that allowed a steeper downdraft angle (50°) for the Keihin FVKD 41mm flat-slide carburettors. The included valve angle went out to 25° and considerable attention was paid to reduce internal friction. There was a 30mm deeper oil pan and larger return oil passages to reduce crankcase pressure. The crankcases were stronger, as were the output shaft and gearbox bearings. Kawasaki's Racing Group also designed the chassis with racing in mind. The frame's main spar size was increased, as was the headstock diameter, and there was a new hollow-cast swingarm pivot plate. There was a claimed increase of 30 per cent in frame rigidity with 1kg less weight and, according to Peter Doyle, 'for the first time it wasn't necessary to brace the frame for racing, although the factory bikes still braced the frame and swingarm to gauge any improvement.' Complementing the chassis improvement was wind tunnel-developed bodywork, with twin ram-air intakes, the fairing being 60mm narrower than before. The six-piston AP brakes and Öhlins suspension were similar to that of the previous year.

After being courted by Suzuki for their World Superbike effort, and making it obvious he intended to pursue a GP career, Gobert was surprised when Muzzy matched Suzuki's $US1.2 million offer. It appeared to be double what he was worth, and joining Gobert was New Zealander Simon Crafar. Although both twins and fours were limited to 162kg this year, the ZX-7RR wasn't as competitive as expected. While the new chassis was an improvement the bikes were initially slower than the final 1995 version. Although acknowledged masters of combustion chamber design the shorter stroke

DOUG CHANDLER

Like Eddie Lawson and Wayne Rainey before him, John Doug Chandler was another product of the California dirt-track school. Born in Salinas on 27 September 1965, Chandler started racing a Honda Mini-Trail at short-tracks at the age of six. He graduated to 80s, then 250s, became a four-time minibike champion, and by 1983 was contesting the Camel Pro Series straight after graduating from high school. He won his first National at the Santa Fe short-track within a month of debut and went on to become 'Rookie of the Year'. Signed by Honda, and requiring more points for the Grand National Championship, he decided to give road racing a try, entering his first event on a Honda RS500 during 1984. Honda downsized its dirt-track effort for 1985, but Chandler continued to ride dirt on privateer Hondas for the next four years, winning eight dirt-track Nationals. He also rode a factory Honda VFR Superbike as a 'B-Team' rider. When Muzzy left Honda as technical manager he signed Chandler, surprising many because Chandler had finished few road races on the Honda and had attracted little attention. Chandler won his first National road race at the end of 1989, joining a select group of only four riders to have won the AMA Grand Slam – scoring victories in mile, half-mile, TT, short-track, and road race Nationals.

After winning the AMA Superbike title on the Muzzy ZX-7, Chandler then headed for Europe, initially racing a Yamaha for Kenny Roberts before switching to Suzuki, and then Cagiva. Chandler achieved six podiums in Grands Prix but Cagiva's retirement at the end of 1994 saw him back in the USA on the Harley-Davidson VR1000 Superbike. For 1996 he was back in the Muzzy Kawasaki squad taking his second AMA title in a spectacular comeback as he hadn't won a major race in nearly six years. Repeating this victory in 1997, Chandler remained Kawasaki's leading Superbike rider in the USA through until 2001.

Left: Doug Chandler has been Kawasaki's most successful Superbike racer, winning three AMA Superbike titles. He took his second championship in 1996 on the Muzzy ZX-7RR. *(Cycle World)*

Opposite top: Anthony Gobert was the sensation at the final World Superbike round in 1994 but failed to deliver during 1995. This is at Hockenheim with a twin exhaust set-up. *(Two Wheels)*

Opposite bottom: Gobert rode the 1995 ZXR750R to victory in its final race, proving that on the right day and in the right hands it was still a race winner. This was the final version of a design that had its origins back in the H1 model of 1989. *(Australian Motorcycle News)*

provided more problems than it solved. The inlet ports were also too large, as were the 41mm carburettors, and although the power was still around 155bhp it was a peakier delivery. During the year, smaller 39mm carburettors were tried, as well as welded and reported cylinder heads, but the lack of development definitely affected the confidence of the team.

The season started poorly when Gobert's victory at Misano was disallowed for the use of a taper insert in front of the carburettor. Gobert didn't win again until Laguna Seca but in the meantime, Crafar notched some consistent results, including a second at Donington. After Gobert broke his collarbone during qualifying in Indonesia he lost interest, not returning until the final round in Australia where he won both races. In the meantime Crafar continued to accumulate points, eventually finishing seventh, just ahead of Gobert in the final standings. This year also marked the decline of Muzzy's influence in the World Superbike programme. Towards the end of the season, Muzzy moved his workshop from Germany to Spain, and already there was pressure from the Europeans for a more direct involvement.

Above: New Zealand rider Simon Crafar joined the Muzzy team for 1996, his more consistent performances seeing him ahead of Gobert in the final World Superbike standings. *(Ian Falloon)*

Right: There was a new 750 for 1996, the ZX-7RR, with a stronger frame and an engine with an even shorter stroke. This design formed the basis of Kawasaki Superbikes for the next few years. *(Australian Motorcycle News)*

EUROPEAN, JAPANESE AND AUSTRALIAN SUPERBIKE CHAMPIONSHIPS

While Rob Rhillis was racing in Europe it was left to Aaron Slight to represent TKA in Australia during 1990 and 1991. Slight joined the team back in 1989, playing second fiddle to Phillis, and had one race win that year. The 1990 season then started well for Slight until he crashed a factory ZX-7R Formula 1 bike at the Suzuka Eight-hour race, badly damaging his right hand. As there was doubt he would ride in 1991 Slight missed a World Superbike berth but rewarded Kawasaki with a devastating season in Australia. He won nearly every Australian Superbike race, and all six races in the Pan Pacific Superbike Championship. In Britain too Kawasaki was making a comeback, and while he didn't win any races in the 750cc TT F1 series, John Reynolds was a front-runner on the Team Green ZXR750R.

With Slight moving to World Superbike for 1992 Peter Doyle signed 19-year-old star Matthew Mladin to head the Kawasaki challenge in Australia. Mladin was given an opportunity to ride an ex-factory ZXR-7 in the 1991 Phillip Island Six-hour Endurance race and held second place until the suspension failed. He was even more impressive in the Australian Superbike Championship, his first 12 starts netting 11 victories. So dominant was Mladin's performance that he earned a Cagiva 500 Grand Prix ride for 1993. In the UK, former motocross rider John Reynolds won the 750cc Supercup with nine victories. He also took the *MCN* Superbike Challenge with two rounds remaining on the Team Green ZXR750R.

Without a ride in World Superbike, Rob Phillis returned to Australia for 1993 but had a disappointing year, finishing third. There were also problems for Kawasaki in the UK. Following a 34 per cent sales slump during 1992, the successful Team Green Team was disbanded, the ZXR750R being taken over by Brian Morrison. However, it was Medd Racing's Ray Stringer who gave Kawasaki their best result, with a third in the TT Superbike Supercup and a fifth in the British Championship.

After disappointment in Europe, Mladin returned to Australia to race for TKA in 1994. This time though he couldn't repeat his 1992 result. Even though he won eight races, crashes and retirements saw him third, behind Kawasaki privateer Martin Craggill. Mladin came second in 1995 and only in Germany did Kawasaki have any success that year, Jochen Schmid winning the German Pro-Superbike Championship. For 1996, Kawasaki Motors UK re-entered the British Superbike Championship with two riders, Terry Rymer and Iain MacPherson. However, although there were a few respectable results it was an inauspicious return for Kawasaki.

After a few lean years Martin Craggill gave the ZX-7RR victory in the Australian Superbike Championship in 1997, also winning the Shell Superbike series that year. He repeated this in 1998 while Chris Walker came second in the British Superbike Championship, with five race wins. Walker again came second (with three race wins) in the 1999 British Superbike Championship, while Andrew Pitt was second in Australia. There was also a serious attempt mounted on the 1999 All-Japan Superbike Championship, with three riders: Takeishi, Tamaki Serizawa, and Hitoyasu Izutsu. Serizawa finished sixth overall. This bore fruit when Izutsu won this championship in 2000. The same year also saw Giovanni Bussei victorious in the Italian Superbike Championship with three victories on the Bertocchi ZX-7RR, and Swiss rider Paul Leuthard won the German Pro Superbike title. The ZX-7RR may have struggled in World Superbike but it was still surprisingly competitive in these National Championships.

Martin Craggill dominated Australian Superbike racing during 1997 and 1998 on the Team Kawasaki Australia ZX-7RR. *(Australian Motorcycle News)*

1997

Right: Former Grand Prix team manager Harald Eckl was hired to run the factory World Superbike Team for 1997. *(Ian Falloon)*

Below: The 1997 World Superbike racer was a significantly improved machine, Yanagawa winning two races in this series during that year. *(Australian Motorcycle News)*

There was a major restructuring of the factory Superbike team for 1997. Kawasaki Germany became directly involved, hiring former 250cc German Champion Harald Eckl as team manager. After an approach in August, Eckl was slow to sign, and it wasn't until November 1996 that the team was set up in Eckl's home town, Vohenstrauss. Operating with a more generous budget, Simon Crafar provided the link with the previous season, and was now joined by Japanese rider Akira Yanagawa. New crankcases allowed for the installation of the gear camshaft drive available in the customer racing kit, and there was a new factory cylinder head, camshafts and two-ring slipper pistons. The con-rods and valves were titanium and there was new programmable digital ignition. With a 14:1 compression ratio and an Akrapovic exhaust system, the power was around 158bhp at 14,000rpm. There were new Öhlins 46mm forks, a shorter, stiffer and lighter swingarm with a different linkage, and 320mm four-piston Brembo front brakes to replace the AP. Wheels were Marchesini, generally a 3.50x17-inch front and 6.00x16.5-inch rear, shod as usual with Dunlop tyres. In addition to the Kawasaki Racing Team, Piergiorgio Bontempi rode a semi-supported ZX-7RR for Bertocchi. Bontempi ran a 1996 engine until Albacete, where he received updated components.

Although there was only limited development, and few new parts, the ZX-7RR surprised everyone at the beginning of the season as results were much improved over the previous year. The lost speed of 1996 was found, Crafar qualifying fastest at one of the quickest tracks, Hockenheim. Yanagawa then gave Kawasaki their first win of the year at the revamped A1-Ring at Zeltweg. Yanagawa won again in Sugo and, after a miserable season where he had been brought down several times through no fault of his own, Crafar was robbed of victory at Indonesia. Only two corners from the finish John Kocinski crashed into him, bringing them both down and dashing Crafar's hope of a World Superbike victory.

1998

Kawasaki's racing director, Makoto Ohtsu, indicated that 1998 would culminate in Kawasaki's three-year plan to win the World Superbike Championship. The 1997 ZX-7RR had proved the most competitive and promising of the four-cylinder Superbikes, but unfortunately developments for 1998 were a step backwards. No longer a race winner, the ZX-7RR now struggled even to make the podium. To improve acceleration there were new camshafts, ignition, Akrapovic exhaust, and needles for the Keihin 41mm carburettors, but the increased bottom and mid-range power induced wheelspin, leading to tyre and suspension problems. With a 14.7:1 compression ratio the power was increased to 165bhp at 14,500rpm, but this didn't translate into results. Chassis developments included BBS 3.50x17-inch and 6.00x6.5-inch wheels and new Öhlins suspension, with the older style two-pad Brembo four-piston front brake calipers.

Yanagawa proved a sensation in his first year of World Superbike but the 1998 ZX-7RR was so difficult to ride that he could not challenge the Ducatis and Hondas. Even the new Yamaha R7 was proving more competitive and it wasn't until Laguna Seca that Yanagawa managed a podium finish. However, this also coincided with a serious crash after Chandler's sliding Muzzy ZX-7RR took him out halfway through the race. Initially diagnosed with possible spinal damage, amazingly Yanagawa came back two rounds later, at the A1-Ring, to claim second on the grid. He then finished second in the final race of the year at Sugo. Replacing Crafar was British rider Neil Hodgson who also struggled to come to terms with the difficult ZX-7RR. Hodgson's best result was a fourth at Monza, and with Yanagawa ending seventh and Hodgson 11th overall it was one of Kawasaki's most disappointing years ever in World Superbike.

British rider Neil Hodgson partnered Yanagawa in Eckl's team for 1998, but the ZX-7RR was so difficult to ride that good results were difficult.
(Ian Falloon)

As a factory rider since 1997, Akira Yanagawa has shouldered the burden of racing a sometimes uncompetitive machine.

(Ian Falloon)

AKIRA YANAGAWA

When Akira Yanagawa joined Eckl's Kawasaki Team for 1997 he was virtually unknown outside Japan. Even there he had not figured prominently but he made an immediate impression in Europe, becoming the first Japanese rider to win a non-Japanese round of the World Superbike Championship. Yanagawa was born on 15 July 1971 in Kagoshima, and began racing a Honda NSR 50 mini-bike during 1987. Success during 1988 saw him move to the 250 Sports Production Championship in 1989 and in 1990, he won the Japanese Formula 3, 250 Production, and 250 Club championships. He then raced in 250cc GP and for 1992, was offered a factory Suzuki in the All-Japan F1 Championship. Drafted into the Kawasaki Racing Team during 1995, Yanagawa finished sixth in the All-Japan Superbike Championship. One of the most approachable and genial of all racers, Yanagawa has been Kawasaki's leading World Superbike rider since 1997, but for 2002, returned to Japan to assist in the development of the new GP1 venture.

AMA SUPERBIKE RACING 1996–2001

By 1996, the AMA Superbike Championship was a considerably more professional series than it was back in 1991 when Doug Chandler left to pursue a GP career. There were now six factory-backed teams with 13 factory riders and Chandler battled all season with the Honda of Miguel DuHamel. Chandler won at Laguna Seca, sealing the Championship by a mere five points at the final round at Las Vegas.

At Daytona, 1997, the Muzzy ZX-7RR Superbikes featured a single-sided RAM cast-magnesium swingarm and the engines finally produced more power than they had in 1995. After finishing a strong second at Daytona Chandler then went on to his only win at Laguna Seca, his consistency seeing him win a second straight AMA Superbike Championship.

For 1998, the Muzzy Superbike featured six-piston AP brake calipers and reverted to a standard-style swingarm. Apart from smaller intake ports and new camshafts engine developments were minimal, and while Chandler failed to win a race his consistent finishes saw him runner-up in the Championship. Chandler again rode the Muzzy ZX-7RR in 1999, this year being joined by Aaron Yates. Early in the season, the ZX-7RR struggled for horsepower but consistent development saw Chandler win three races towards the end of the year (Loudon, Mid-Ohio and Pikes Peak) . He finished fourth overall but this was the final season for Muzzy and Kawasaki, and after 14 seasons Muzzy was told the Road Racing Team would be going in-house.

Under the direction of former jet ski racing manager Michael Preston, Chandler was re-signed along with Eric Bostrom for 2000. Gary Medley returned as Chandlers' crew chief, with Al Ludington wrenching for Bostrom. With Öhlins suspension and Brembo brakes the ZX-7RRs were closer to World Superbike specification and while Bostrom easily adapted to the machine, Chandler struggled. Only Bostrom managed a victory during the season, winning the penultimate round at Pikes Peak to finish fourth overall. Both riders returned for 2001, Bostrom winning at Loudon and Laguna Seca. He also overshadowed the Eckl factory bikes at the Laguna World Superbike round and remained a contender for the AMA Championship, finishing second overall.

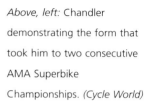

1999

After the dismal 1998 season, continual refinement of the ZX-7RR again saw it become the leading inline four-cylinder Superbike. Development by Kawasaki engineers saw a more linear power curve, similar to the 1997 version, but with a 500rpm increase and more power. New regulations banned titanium valves, but there were now 15:1 two-ring pistons, a rebalanced crankshaft, altered ports and ignition, and a revised Akrapovic exhaust system. There was also a dry clutch, Eckl choosing an Austrian Eskil Suter multi-plate slipper type in preference to the factory clutch. Although now the only team still running carburettors, the power delivery was smoother, and peak power was 168bhp at 14,500rpm.

Chassis development included new Öhlins forks that incorporated the older, 46mm staunchions in the 42mm sliders, and radial Brembo front brake calipers. The BBS wheels were now a 3.5x16.5-inch on the front and 6.00x17-inch on the rear, although problems with Japanese Dunlop tyres early in the season saw an improved British-made 16.5-inch rear Dunlop. With

Opposite: Yanagawa on the 2000 model ZX-7RR. Although he didn't win any races this year he was still very consistent. *(Ian Falloon)*

Below: Developments of the ZX-7RR for 1999 included Öhlins forks with radial Brembo front brake calipers and the machine was much improved over the previous season. *(Ian Falloon)*

essentially the same chassis as the 1996 version, the ZX-7RR was still slightly disadvantaged by its long wheelbase of 1,420mm (55.9in), and a reasonably slow steering of a 24.5° steering head angle and 92mm of trail.

Gregorio Lavilla replaced Hodgson in the Eckl squad but both riders struggled early in the season. However, by Albacete the tyre problems seemed resolved when Yanagawa posted two second places, as well as fastest lap. Yanagawa continued to rack up rostrum finishes (nine in total), culminating in his only victory of the year, the second race at Sugo. This consistency earned him fifth in the Championship while Lavilla finished eighth.

Despite now being in its fifth racing season, the essential excellence of the ZX-7RR design continued to be vindicated during 2000. Engine developments included a further reduction in internal friction, new cylinder head porting and a revised combustion chamber, but retaining steel valves and twin valve springs. The conrods were still titanium, and the two-ring pistons gave a slightly higher compression. There was also a new Akrapovic exhaust with stainless steel header pipes and a titanium collector and muffler. All this combined to see the power increase to 172bhp at 14,800rpm, with the engine safe to 15,000rpm, and more mid-range

After being impressive on a privately run Ducati during 1998, Gregorio Lavilla earned a ride with Eckl's team from 1999. This is Lavilla during 2000, a season interrupted by injury, although his performances during 2001 were much improved.

(Ian Falloon)

power. The ZX-7RR was now the highest revving Superbike, and one of the fastest with a top speed of 198mph (318km/h) recorded at Hockenheim.

Eckl also decided to switch from Öhlins to White Power suspension, the front forks having huge aluminium (rather than the Öhlins steel) 50mm staunchions. The new suspension components were initially quite different to setup but Eckl was assisted here by expert tester Peter Goddard, substituting for an injured Lavilla. A slightly longer swingarm (increasing the wheelbase to 1,440mm/56.7in) altered the weight distribution, now putting 55 per cent on the front wheel, and the effective steering head angle steepened through rear ride height and fork length. To reduce gyroscopic effect the front brake discs were reduced in diameter to 305mm, still with radial Brembo calipers.

The Dunlop tyres were 16.5-inch front and rear, with a slightly wider (6.25-inch) rear wheel.

There were no changes to the Eckl team for 2000, but it was the Japanese rider Hitoyasu Izutsu who upstaged the regular World Superbike runners when he took victory in both races at the third round at Sugo. Izutsu was on a Japanese Kawasaki Racing Team machine, ostensibly similar to the Fuchs-sponsored ZX-7RRs but with Öhlins suspension. Yanagawa came back to take two third places at Monza, and a second at Hockenheim. Replacement Peter Goddard put in some respectable performances until Lavilla returned to celebrate a second place at Oschersleben. Again, Yanagawa's consistency provided him with fifth overall, while Lavilla ended tenth after missing four rounds.

2001–

Easily the oldest design, and one of only two factory four-cylinder machines left competing in World Superbike, there were few changes to the ZX-7RR. Yanagawa and Lavilla remained with the Eckl team, assisted by Izutsu (still with Öhlins rather than White Power suspension) in seven rounds. The season started well, with Lavilla achieving several podium finishes, but Harald Eckl was still unhappy with the regulations that seemingly favoured twin-cylinder machines. 'Kawasaki have always been loyal to the in-line four, and that is how it will stay in Superbike,' Eckl said. Fortunately for Eckl, a change in the regulations for 2002 will give the ZX-7RR a reprieve. For 2002 the four-cylinder machines received a weight reduction to 159kg with the twins' weight increased to 164kg. The return of Yanagawa to Japan also saw a change in the rider line-up for 2002, Izutsu and former Kawasaki UK rider Chris Walker making up the team.

The future for racing and Kawasaki looks promising. With the a new four-stroke GP1 class for 2002, and promise of a full 1,000cc World Superbike category class, regardless of the number of cylinders, set for 2003 or 2004, Kawasaki could again be at the top of the podium.

The 2001 World Superbike racer undressed. This was ostensibly similar to that of the previous year but remained as fast as any of the four-cylinder machines.
(Ian Falloon)

Hitoyasu Izutsu surprised many with two victories during the 2000 season and raced in selected World Superbike events during 2001. *(Ian Falloon)*

INDEX

P

Pace, John 74
Paillot, Thierry 128
Pajic, Mile 120
Palm Beach 85
Palomo, Victor 58
Pan Pacific Cup 32, 43
Pan Pacific Superbike
  Championship 149
Paris 12, 16
Parlotti, Gilberto 16
Paul Ricard 64, 76, 78, 106, 109, 114, 120
Peckett and McNab 76
Pellandini, Sergio 87
Performance team 78, 82, 87, 110-111
Perry, Rick 62, 74, 95, 132
Perth 32
Peyre, John-Bernard 76
Phase One 127
Philippine Grand Prix 26
Phillip Island 66, 127, 135, 146, 149
Phillis, Rob 74, 96, 119-120, 122, 125, 127, 131-132, 134-135, 137-140, 149
Picotte, Pascal 137
Pierce, Ron 57-58, 85, 93-94
Pietermaritzburg 96
Pikes Peak 152
Pipart 76
Pistoni, Pete 88
Pitt, Andrew 144-145, 149
Plumlee, Merlyn 136
Pocono 24, 28, 38, 77-78, 89
Pogue, Sid 80
Polen, Doug 125, 132, 136, 139
Pomona 137
Powerbike International 64
Preston, Michael 152
Pridmore, Reg 77
Prince Albert 80
Prostar Top Fuel/Funnybike
  Championship 82

Q

Quarterley, Dale 137
Quebec 37
Queensland 96

R

Race of the South 61
Rainey, Wayne 85-86, 88-89, 147
Ramsey 11
Ravel, Christian 22
Rayborn, Cal 16
Read, Phil 13, 61, 64, 94
Reggiani, Loris 111
Reid, Dick 15
Renouf 71

Revé Racing 146
Reynolds, John 144, 146, 149
Rhodesia 96
Rice, Steve 80, 82
Rieder, Martin 128
Riverside 58, 85-86, 94
Road America 136
Road Atlanta race 28, 32, 38, 41, 78, 137, 141
Roberts, Kenny 24, 41, 53, 64, 98, 147
Roche, Raymond 82, 87, 132
Rooyan, Gerry van 87
Rosset, Serge 82, 87
Rossi, Achille 26
Rossi, Graziano 102
Royal Air Force 50
Rubatto-Lortz 144
Ruiz, Roger 76
Rungis 12
Russell, Scott 125, 127, 131, 134, 136-142, 144, 146
Rymer, Terry 119, 125, 127-128, 142, 149
Ryo, Akira 125

S

Sachsenring 14
Sacramento 43
Saito, Sid 36
Salinas 147
Salisbury 96
Salzburg 146
Salzburg Grand Prix 26
Samin, Pierre-Etienne 120, 122
San Carlos 57
Santa Ana 28, 57, 85
Sarron, Christian 74, 97
Sato, Nagato 91, 94
Sayle, Murray 43-45, 53, 62, 74, 93-95, 97
Scarborough 15, 53, 61-62
Scarnato, Sébastien 128
Schlögl, Sepp 97, 101, 104, 106, 109, 111
Schmid, Jochen 146, 149
Schwantz, Kevin 141
Scott, Gary 41
Sears Point 20, 77, 86, 88, 137
Seattle 85
Sebileau, Bertrand 128-129
Seeley, Colin 32, 33
Sellers, Harold 25, 31, 41
Serizawa, Tamaki 125, 149
Shah Alam 112, 135
Sheene, Barry 16, 52-53, 58-59, 61, 64
Shell Superbike series 149
Shenton, Stan 43, 50, 54, 57, 64, 93-94, 96-97, 102
Shenton, Stuart 50, 102, 113-114, 117
Shetler, Jeff 40, 51, 67

Shin Etsu 134
Sibille, Roger 120
Sidemm 66, 71-74
Silverstone 58, 91, 97, 101-102, 105-106, 109-110, 114, 117
Simmonds, Dave 11-16, 19, 22, 26, 30-31
Simmonds, Jennie 12
Simmonds, John 12
Simmonds, Violet 12
Simul, Michel 120, 127
Singapore Grand Prix 15
Skamser, Red 25
Slight, Aaron 112, 120, 125, 127, 134, 138-140, 142, 149
Smart, Paul 24-25, 31-33, 36
Smith, Bill 15, 22
Smith, Dave 20, 22
Smith, Mike 144
Smith, Tim 40, 57
Snetterton 15, 61, 114
Sohwa, Takahiro 120, 122, 134-135, 137-138
South Africa 96
South African Championships 96
South African Grand Prix 112
Spa Francorchamps 14, 74, 87, 114, 120, 127-128
Spain 14, 26, 62, 97-98, 111, 138, 140, 148
Spanish Grand Prix 11, 16, 31, 106
Spencer, Freddie 77, 85
Sprayson, Ken 26
Starr, Dale 77
Steele, Mike 74
Steven, Michel 120
Stevens, Thomas 136, 144
Stöllinger, Edi 91, 102
Stringer, Ray 149
Sugo 120, 122, 125, 132, 134-135, 138, 140, 150-151, 154, 156
Suter, Eskil 153
Suzuka 40, 96, 128
Suzuka Eight-hour race 78, 88, 96, 119-120, 122, 125, 127-128, 138-139, 141, 149
Suzuki 11, 13-14, 16, 26, 32, 36, 45, 52-54, 57-59, 64, 66, 78, 96, 104, 114, 125, 127, 137, 141, 146-147, 152
Suzuki, Ken 50, 97, 113
Sweden 54, 117
Swedish Grand Prix (TT) 31, 52, 94, 97, 101-102
Switzerland 73
Sydney 45, 74

T

Tada, Kiyokazu 120, 122
Tait, Percy 72
Takeishi, Shinya 125, 149

Talladega 22, 28, 32, 34, 36, 38, 41, 43, 78, 85
Tamura, Ichiro 113
Tanaguchi 14
Tasmania 131
Team Bolliger Switzerland 129
Team Boyer Kawasaki 34, 43, 48, 50-52, 58, 64, 93-94, 96
Team Green 122, 149
Team Hansen 24-26, 31, 33, 59
Team Kawasaki 36, 38, 51, 61, 97, 120
Team Kawasaki Australia (TKA) 43, 45, 57, 61, 66-67, 97, 112, 120, 131-132, 134-135, 138-139, 142, 149
Texas 136
Thruxton 400-mile race 43, 50, 64, 72, 96
Thruxton 500-mile race 19
Thuett, Shell 88
Thunderbike Trophy 144
Tohatsu 12, 50
Tokyo 12
Toland, Doug 127
Toombs, Ron 40, 43-45, 66
Tournadre, Jean-Louis 110
Trett, Elmer 82
Triumph 29, 31-32, 50, 53, 59
Tsukamoto, Shouichi 120, 122, 125, 140
Tsuruta, Ryuji 122, 125
TT F1 and Superbike 149
Tuxworth, Neil 12

U

Uchida, Michio 50
UK 82, 97, 144, 149
Ulster Grand Prix 13, 22
USA 16, 19-20, 22, 25-26, 28, 36-37, 40, 45, 47, 50-51, 53, 57, 67, 77, 80, 82, 88, 93-94, 96, 109, 134, 136-138, 144-145

V

van Vaerenbergh, Johan 120
Vance and Hines 89
Venezuela 47, 57-58, 98
Vesco, Don 80
Vial, Alain 72, 74
Victoria 45
Victorian TT 15, 31
Vieira, Alex 119-120, 127
Villa, Walter 38
Vincent, Chris 12, 15
Vink, Henk 20, 80
Vohenstrauss 150
Vukmanovich, George 40-41, 43

W

Wada, Mashiro 37-38, 45, 53, 61,

97
Wagga 132
Walker, Chris 128, 149, 157
Weber, Emil 132
WERA 141
West German Grand Prix 94
White, Ralph 16, 26, 29
Whitelock, Steve 24-25, 31-32, 36
Williams, Charlie 54
Williams, Peter 33
Willing, Len 131
Willoughby District Motorcycle
  Club 74
Willow Springs 16, 24, 31
Wilvert, Hurley 24, 32, 36-38, 40-41, 43-45, 71
Wolff, Thad 86
Work, Bob 61
World Championship, Formula 750 45
World Championships, 500, 350, 250, 125cc 67, 74, 88-89, 91, 96-98, 101-102, 104, 105-106, 110-112, 144
World Endurance
  Championship 78, 82, 87, 89, 119-120, 122, 127-129
World Series 66, 114
World Superbike
  Championship 45, 132-134, 137-143, 146, 148-152, 154-155, 157
World Supersport Championship 144-145
World TT Formula One 53, 78, 82, 120, 122, 127, 132

Y

Yamaha 13-14, 16, 24, 37, 40, 51-54, 57-58, 61, 64, 66-68, 88, 93-94, 96, 98, 104-105, 110, 141, 151
Yamamoto-san 145
Yanagawa, Akira 125, 150-152, 154, 156-157
Yates, Aaron 152
Yokohama, Atsushi 12
Yoshida, Kazuhito (Ken) 25, 31, 37, 47
Yoshimura 71-72, 141
Yugoslav Grand Prix 104, 106
Yugoslavia 14, 97, 101, 105
Yurikusa, Misao 47, 50

Z

Zeltweg 150
Zender, Alfons 104
Zolder 120
Zubani, Giamperi 26